PIERRE BOURDIEU

KEY SOCIOLOGISTS
Series Editor: Peter Hamilton
The Open University

KEY SOCIOLOGISTS

Series Editor: PETER HAMILTON
The Open University, Milton Keynes

This series presents concise and readable texts covering the work, life and influence of many of the most important sociologists, and sociologically-relevant thinkers, from the birth of the discipline to the present day. Aimed primarily at the undergraduate, the books will also be useful to pre-university students and others who are interested in the main ideas of sociology's major thinkers.

MARX AND MARXISM
PETER WORSLEY, Professor of Sociology, University of Manchester

MAX WEBER
FRANK PARKIN, Tutor in Politics and Fellow of Magdalen College, Oxford

EMILE DURKHEIM
KENNETH THOMPSON, Reader in Sociology, Faculty of Social Sciences, The Open University, Milton Keynes

TALCOTT PARSONS
PETER HAMILTON, The Open University, Milton Keynes

SIGMUND FREUD
ROBERT BOCOCK, The Open University, Milton Keynes

C. WRIGHT MILLS
J. E. T. ELDRIDGE, Department of Sociology, University of Glasgow

THE FRANKFURT SCHOOL
TOM BOTTOMORE, Emeritus Professor of Sociology, University of Sussex

GEORG SIMMEL
DAVID FRISBY, Department of Sociology, University of Glasgow

KARL MANNHEIM
DAVID KETTLER, Professor of Political Studies, Trent University, Ontario; VOLKER MEJA, Associate Professor of Sociology, Memorial University of Newfoundland, and NICO STEHR, Professor of Sociology, University of Alberta

MICHEL FOUCAULT
BARRY SMART, Department of Sociological Studies, University of Sheffield

THE ETHNOMETHODOLOGISTS
WES SHARROCK and BOB ANDERSON, Department of Sociology, University of Manchester

ERVING GOFFMAN
TOM BURNS, Emeritus Professor of Sociology, University of Edinburgh

JÜRGEN HABERMAS
MICHAEL PUSEY, University of New South Wales, Australia

ROBERT K. MERTON
CHARLES CROTHERS, University of Auckland, New Zealand

PIERRE BOURDIEU

RICHARD JENKINS

Senior Lecturer in Sociology
University College, Swansea

London and New York

First published 1992
by Routledge
11 New Fetter Lane, London EC4P 4EE

Simultaneously published in the USA and Canada
by Routledge
29 West 35th Street, New York, NY 10001

Routledge is an imprint of the Taylor & Francis Group

Reprinted 1993, 1994, 1996, 1998, 1999

Typeset in Times by Intype, London
Printed in England by Clays Ltd, St Ives plc

British Library Cataloguing in Publication Data
A catalogue record for this book is available from the British Library

Library of Congress Cataloguing in Publication Data
Jenkins, Richard, 1952–
    Pierre Bourdieu / Richard Jenkins.
        p.   cm. – (Key sociologists)
    Includes bibliographical references and index.
    1. Bourdieu, Pierre.   2. Sociology–France.
        3. Sociology–Methodology.
    I. Title.   II. Series.
    HM22.F8J46   1992   92–2720
    301′.01–dc20   CIP

Table of Contents

Acknowledgements

This book is the direct product of Chris Rojek's suggestion that I write it. Without that suggestion, it would probably never have seen the light of day; nor might it ever have done so without his unobtrusive but supportive editorial presence. My thanks are also due to Jack Goody, who first introduced me to Bourdieu's work as something which I might find stimulating and interesting. He was right.

I have quoted particularly extensively in the course of the text from two of Bourdieu's books, *Distinction* and *The Logic of Practice*. I gratefully acknowledge permission to do so from, respectively, Routledge and Polity Press/Basil Blackwell Ltd. Les Éditions de Minuit generously granted similar permissions with respect to the non-English language copyright, throughout the world, of the original editions, *La Distinction* and *Le sens pratique*.

I must also thank Stephanie Adams, Kate Ingram, John Parker and Chris Stray, for reading all or part of various versions of the book whilst it was in preparation. Their comments – which I confess I have not always accepted – and, much more important, their encouragement made what sometimes felt like an impossible job seem more manageable. Pierre Bourdieu and Richard Nice were also kind enough to enter into what were for me helpful exchanges of correspondence.

Finally, I must express my admiration for the speed and accuracy with which Letty John typed up what was not a straight-forward manuscript.

1

A Book for Reading

Pierre Bourdieu has, with no doubt conscious irony, referred to his recent study of the French university system, *Homo Academicus*, as a 'book for burning'. As an insider's attempt to distance himself from, demythologise and analyse critically that system, it is, he suggests, vulnerable to colleaguely accusations of subversion or heresy, if not outright treachery. As with most of Bourdieu's work, in particular his work over the last two decades, its subversive potential is, however, considerably undermined by the nature of the language that he uses and his general writing style. Idiosyncratic usages and neologisms, allied to frequently repetitive, long sentences which are burdened down with a host of sub-clauses and discursive detours, combine with complicated diagrams and visual schemes to confront the reader with a task that many, whether they be undergraduates, postgraduates or professional social scientists, find daunting. As the reader will gather from what I have just written, it is not that I have any necessary objections to either longish sentences or sub-clauses. Bourdieu's writing, however, which he has described as 'a permanent struggle against ordinary language',[1] is, as I will argue in a later chapter, unnecessarily long-winded, obscure, complex and intimidatory. He does not have to write in this fashion to say what he wants to say.

In offering this introduction to Bourdieu's work and thought, therefore, my first objective has been to discuss that work and thought outside the opaque language games of his sociological circle and his interpreters. In other words, my intention is to 'translate' Bourdieu into language which is as clear and as straightforward as possible. Hence, this is a 'book for reading'. This objective is informed by two basic propositions: first, that it is *worth* writing such a book, and second, that it is *possible* to do so without doing violence to the subtlety and depth of his arguments.

With respect to the first of these, there can be little doubt that Bourdieu's contributions to sociology and social anthropology are important. With the passing of Althusser, Barthes and Foucault he, more than any other comparable figure – Boudon or Touraine, for example – has come to personify the continued value and vigour of a distinctly French intellectual tradition within the social sciences. Occupying as he does a political and theoretical space constructed out of the divergent currents of Marx, Weber and Durkheim, structuralism and interactionism, pessimistic determinism and a celebratory belief in the improvisatory creative potential of human practice, he appears to be an attractive and heterodox source of inspiration for social theory in the 1990s.

There are a number of more specific reasons why Bourdieu's work is so important. First, there is the major contribution which he has made to the debate about the relationship between structure and action which re-emerged during the late 1970s and early 1980s as the key question for social theory. Second, and by interesting comparison with, say, Anthony Giddens, that contribution has consistently been framed by an engagement between systematic empirical work – whether relying on ethnography or social survey approaches – and reflexive theorising. It is the tension between these two aspects of Bourdieu's work that makes it so interesting: 'theory without empirical research is empty, empirical research without theory is blind'.[2] Third, and as a consequence, perhaps, of the fact that Bourdieu has been an active social researcher throughout his career, epistemological questions about the nature of adequate sociological knowledge and the conditions under which it is possible are central to his project. These are questions of which many sociologists and anthropologists – whether they see themselves as primarily 'theorists' or 'researchers' – have, to the detriment of their enterprise, lost sight.

Finally – although it would be possible to provide further justifications for writing a short introduction to his work – Bourdieu is, by virtue of the three points mentioned above, enormously good to think with. His work invites, even demands, argument and reflection. If one makes the initial effort, it is, I suspect, impossible to remain neutral about what he is saying. Whether one agrees with him or not there is something to be learned, something to be turned to good purpose in one's own work, and irritating, persistent problems – creative sociological doubts – which are impossible to ignore. He raises tricky questions and helps to provide some of the means by which they may be answered. Bourdieu's work offers the patient reader a tremendously useful intellectual resource.

> As far as I'm concerned, I have very pragmatic relationships with authors: I turn to them as I would to fellows and craft-masters, in the sense those words had in the mediaeval guild – people you can ask to give you a hand in difficult situations.[3]

It is just such a 'pragmatic relationship' with Bourdieu's writings that I hope to encourage here, a relationship that permits of the most trenchant criticism while recognising the great value of what he has to say.

Such a relationship is all the more necessary because, until fairly recently, the appropriation of Bourdieu's work in the English-speaking world has been problematic. Because of the difficulty of his work, and also perhaps because of the uses to which the esoteric writings of a particular species of French intellectual can be put in the accumulation of cultural capital in certain areas of Anglophone academic life, Bourdieu has been more read about than read, more talked about than critically discussed. Some of his books – *Reproduction in Education, Society and Culture* is probably the best example – are very widely cited. By comparison with authors such as Barthes or Foucault, however, the critical literature dealing with Bourdieu is relatively sparse, although this lack is now beginning to be remedied.[4] What is more, on looking at the uses to which a text such as *Reproduction* has been put in the work of English-speaking writers, one often comes away with the impression that their knowledge and understanding of it are, at best, superficial.[5]

This, however, may be a shortcoming of more than just the Anglophone world. Martine Segalen, for example, has recently discussed Bourdieu's influence upon French ethnology. She defines 'strategies', a key concept in Bourdieu's analytical framework, as 'the product of social rules where demographic variables and economic and "symbolic" capital intervene'.[6] As we will see later, to conceptualise *strategies* in terms of *rules* could not be further from the truth of Bourdieu's model.

A further problem is the fact that much of the discussion of Bourdieu concentrates on a fairly narrow spectrum of his work. Very few critiques span the full range – from Algerian ethnography to the sociology of education to methodology – or even a substantial slice of it. This, of course, may be understandable. Bourdieu's vision is broader and his scholarship more substantial than most of those, and I include myself in this, who write about him. It is a critical narrowness, however, which has unfortunately encouraged a less than adequate appreciation of what he is saying. It does Bourdieu a considerable injustice, for example, to regard him as primarily a sociologist of education or culture. There is much more to the man than this.

An example of this kind of tunnel vision can be found in social anthropologist Maurice Bloch's discussion of Bourdieu's structuralist analysis of the Kabyle house (a paper which is discussed in detail in Chapter Two). It is really only possible for Bloch to argue that Bourdieu's model of the socialisation process is unidimensional and inadequate – i.e. making no allowances for ideology[7] – by virtue of his apparent ignorance of Bourdieu's extensive, but nominally sociological, analyses of the French education system.

As a consequence, therefore, of superficiality, narrowness of focus or disciplinary fastidiousness one often encounters Bourdieu in other people's writing as either a straw man or an idol without feet of clay. With the exception of his work on sport, I intend to make an attempt here to remedy this situation by dealing with all of Bourdieu's *oeuvre*. In particular, I hope to convince the reader of the centrality to sociology and anthropology – certainly inasmuch as they are intellectual enterprises necessarily rooted in empirical research – of Bourdieu's approach to epistemology and methodology. To reiterate my earlier point about 'being good to think with', his significance in this respect lies not so much in whether one accepts or rejects his arguments, but in the fact that he makes them at all.

This book, therefore, has three objectives: first, to produce a properly critical account of Bourdieu's work which will be accessible to students; second, in doing so, to examine a broad range of Bourdieu's work; and third, to place Bourdieu's epistemological and methodological writings at the centre of that account. Before going on to tackle this agenda, however, it may be useful to situate his work in its proper context, his personal biography and intellectual career.

LIFE AND WORK

On many occasions, particularly during interviews, Bourdieu has talked about the relationship between his experience and history as a person and his intellectual project. Although he now occupies the most senior chair in sociology in France, at the *Collège de France*, he has come to it in a roundabout fashion. According to his most faithful English translator, Richard Nice, there is a myth – that of 'the peasant boy confronting urban civilisation' – and there is a more serious version of Bourdieu's life, that of a 'petit bourgeois and a success story'.[8] One can perhaps hear echoes of that romantic myth when Bourdieu says things such as, 'I didn't have any accounts to settle with the bourgeois family'.[9] More directly, later in the same interview, in discussing his break with the 'arrogance and distance' which characterises the relationship between anthropology and its subject matter – people – he suggests that:

> The difficulties I had in studying Kabyle peasants, their marriage patterns or rites, 'from above' is surely related to my encounter, as a child, with peasants whose views on such matters as honour or dishonour were in no form different from my own.[10]

Insofar as they are of any importance, here are some bare facts to begin with. Born in Denguin, a small town in the Béarn area of the Département des Basses-Pyrenées in south-eastern France, on 1 April 1930, Pierre Bourdieu is the son of a civil servant, *un fonctionnaire*. More petit bourgeois than peasant, perhaps, but it was a rural area and close to the land. In the early 1950s he attended the *École normale supérieure* in Paris, an elite teacher training college. Although he graduated as an *agrégé de philosophie*, he refused to write a thesis in reaction, by his own account, to the pedestrian and authoritarian nature of the education which was on offer. It was not only the institution, however, with which he (and others) were uncomfortable:

> The pressure exerted by Stalinism was so exasperating that, around 1951, we had founded at the École normale (with Bianco, Comte, Marin, Derrida, Patiente and others) a Committee for the Defence of Freedom, which Le Roy Ladurie denounced in the communist cell at the École . . .[11]

For a year following his *agrégation* he taught in a provincial *lycée*. Then, in 1956, he was conscripted, serving for two years with the French Army in Algeria. It was this experience more than any other which appears to mark the beginning of his journey from philosophy to the social sciences. It was also a political experience:

> After two arduous years during which there was no possibility of doing research I could do some work again. I began to write a book with the intention of high-lighting the plight of the Algerian people and, also, that of the French settlers whose situation was no less dramatic . . . I was appalled by the gap between the views of French intellectuals about this war and how it should be brought to an end, and my own experiences . . . Maybe I wanted to be useful in order to overcome my guilty conscience about merely being a participant observer in this appalling war.[12]

The book was *Sociologie de l'Algérie*, first published in 1958,[13] and for two further years Bourdieu stayed in Algeria, teaching at the University of Algiers and undertaking additional field research. He has described this, his first book, as 'the poor attempt of an outsider'; be that as it may, it now, with the benefit of hindsight, appears to sit outside the subsequent developmental stream of his career. Very much a work of empirical social investigation, it offers, even yet, a wealth of information about Algeria and its peoples but little in the way of analysis. It was, nonetheless, a beginning and it provided him with useful research experience.

On his return to France in 1960 he spent a year as an *assistant* in the Faculty of Arts at the University of Paris. Having become something of an anthropologist, albeit a self-taught one, he attended Lévi-Strauss's seminars at the *Collège de France* and ethnology lectures at the *Musée de l'Homme*. He also returned to reading Marx and worked as Raymond Aron's assistant. Now it was sociology which beckoned.

Following three years at the University of Lille he returned to Paris in 1964, as Director of Studies at *l'École pratique des hautes etudes*, the Parisian power base upon which his subsequent career was initially founded. From this point on we witness an ever-gathering momentum of research activity and publication. A research grouping began to accrete around Bourdieu; in the rarefied intellectual cockpit of Paris he became a *patron*. In particular, there was the foundation in 1968 of the *Centre de Sociologie Européenne*, of which he remains the Director, and the subsequent launch of its associated journal, *Actes de la recherche en sciences sociales*, an innovative academic publishing venture which mixed text, photographs and illustrations in a refreshing and, until relatively recently, unique style. There are also a number of long-standing collaborators – Boltanski, Darbel, de St Martin and Passeron, to name only some – with whom Bourdieu has worked on what is obviously a programmatic and, to a degree, collective enterprise. There seems little doubt, however, that he is the driving force, much more than a first among equals:

> I see the research group as a very little group, in comparison with others. Also the people who work with me are very modest. There are some of us who think that it is a strength of the group that they work so much, and that they are also so modest. They will accept and do things that arrogant people would not do and that is very important.[14]

There is an intriguing ambiguity in the above – a mixture of humility about the task in hand and (possibly) arrogance about his role in that task – which might be diagnostic or indicative of his whole project. The one tempers the other to create a sociology that is never less than fascinating.

In 1981, following various episodes of internal politics in the wake of Raymond Aron's retirement, and in competition with Boudon and Touraine, Bourdieu was appointed to the chair at the *Collège de France*. He continues to run the Centre for European Sociology and to research and to publish profusely. Whether he was originally a peasant or a petit-bourgeois, he has arrived; there is, in terms of the institutions of French education, nowhere to which he may further aspire. It has been a long journey from fieldwork in Algeria to the *Collège de France*; in becoming a Professor of Sociology, the anthropologist has finally come all the way home.

Insofar as he is either a sociologist *or* an anthropologist, Bourdieu remains, however, something of a philosopher. Philosophy – or, more accurately, perhaps, a fascination with some of the fundamental problems of philosophy: mind, agency, personhood – has consistently provided him with a theoretical discourse capable of unifying the disparate empirical strands of his work. It is this philosopher's stance towards the world, tempered by the experience of conducting actual research, which lies behind his interest in epistemology and issues of methodology. What is more, it is that research background which enables him, on the other hand, to reject the omniscient pretensions and totalising ambitions of philosophy. Rather than attempting to pronounce on 'the big questions' – 'the meaning of life' – Bourdieu is more interested in how those questions become possible and the manner in which that meaning is practically accomplished as a social phenomenon.

Having summarised something of his biography, what of Bourdieu's intellectual formation? We have already seen him refer to his rejection of both Stalinism and institutional conservatism while a student, and to his exasperation with the French left's understanding of the Algerian war. Elsewhere he has spoken with some feeling of his impatience with intellectual fashions and those who promote them.[15] In the pressurised social field that is *tout Paris* – the self-regarding, somewhat inward-looking world of French intellectual life, a world which perhaps has no Anglophone equivalent, and where these things *matter* [16] – Bourdieu has, in institutional, intellectual and political terms, attempted to plough his own furrow. He may now be one of its brightest stars, but it is in obstinate and ambiguous reaction to the professional and intellectual world of which he is a member (the same impulse which has informed his research into French higher education and cultural taste) that his thinking has developed.

The first important reaction was against the existentialist phenomenology of Sartre, perhaps *the* ascendant school of thought and political stance of the Paris of Bourdieu's student days. Once again, this was, for Bourdieu, a political statement as much as anything else. Commenting subsequently upon Sartre's arguments concerning the transformative power of revolutionary consciousness in *Being and Nothingness*, Bourdieu argues that,

> If the world of action is nothing other than this universe of interchangeable possibles, entirely dependent on the decrees of the consciousness which creates it and hence totally devoid of *objectivity*, if it is moving because the subject chooses to be moved, revolting because he chooses to be revolted, then emotions, passions and actions are merely games of bad faith, sad farces in which one is both bad actor and good audience.[17]

There is, therefore, more to social life than the subjective consciousness of the actors who move within it and produce it. There is, if you like, an objective social reality beyond the immediate interactional sphere and the self-conscious awareness of individuals.

The nature of that 'objective' reality, social structure in Anglo-American sociological usage, is, however, equally problematic. As an apprentice anthropologist Bourdieu came into contact with the other great edifice of post-war French thought, structuralism, in the person of Lévi-Strauss. It is in his reaction to this that the other side of Bourdieu's theoretical dialectic is to be found. In the first instance, and indeed for some time, he worked as a 'blissful structuralist',[18] the apogee of this aspect of his development being his acclaimed analysis of the Kabyle house as a symbolic system.[19] He was motivated to move beyond this by a realisation that the behaviour, the practice, of the people about whom structuralist models were constructed was at variance with the rules of conduct which those models formulated. Structuralism, he began to realise, had little or no explanatory or predictive power:

> It was only after a detour over terrain familiar to myself – on the one hand, life in the Béarn where I come from, and university life on the other – that I uncovered for myself the objective presuppositions of the structuralist approach; one of them being the privileged position accorded to the observer vis-a-vis the native population which, it is assumed, are ineluctably trapped within the unconscious . . . My intention was to bring real-life actors back in who had vanished at the hands of Lévi-Strauss and other structuralists, especially Althusser,

through being considered as epiphenomena of structures.
I do mean 'actors' not 'subjects'. An action is not the
mere carrying out of a rule.[20]

In these two movements – reactions to Sartre and existentialism,
on the one hand, and Lévi-Strauss and structuralism, on the
other – lie the roots of Bourdieu's attempt to overcome the
'absurd opposition between individual and society',[21] the opposition between *subjectivism* and *objectivism*. This he regards as
the key and the ultimate dualistic category which structures and
organises social science and, at the end of the day, the root of
social science's inadequacies. As a principle framing sociological
and anthropological thinking, this opposition derives further
force from its affinity to common-sense notions about the nature
of the social world. His attempt to overcome this fundamental
dualism, through the introduction into his analysis of practice of
notions such as habitus, field and strategy, will be discussed in
subsequent chapters.

There are other ways, of course, to look at the development
of Bourdieu's sociology. Where, for example, does he stand in
relation to the three great 'founding fathers', Marx, Weber and
Durkheim? This may be a very useful question to ask; certainly,
there seems to be some disagreement about the matter. Stuart
Hall, for example, has described him as offering the possibility
of 'an adequate Marxist theory of ideology' by virtue of his
successful synthesis of Marxism and structuralism.[22] For E.P.
Thompson, however, it is as an antidote to the errors of Marxist
structuralism, as exemplified by Althusser, that Bourdieu is to
be recommended.[23] Elsewhere there is another view to be
found: '. . . often erroneously viewed as a Marxist in the Anglo-
Saxon world, Bourdieu is better understood as a sociologist of
philosophical formation deeply influenced by French structuralism and by the works of Max Weber and Emile Durkheim'.[24]
All things to all people, or so it seems. From his own point of
view, the question is both more straightforward and less reasonable: 'whether or not to be a Marxist or a Weberian is a religious
alternative, not a scientific one'.[25] He is on record as objecting
to the question – are you a Marxist or a Weberian? – actually
being posed; it is, he suggests, almost always polemic, 'almost
always a way of reducing, or destroying, you'.[26]

And, indeed, looking at his work it is quite clear that, posed
as alternatives, the choice between Marx, Weber or Durkheim

makes little sense. From Marx, particularly the early Marx of the *Theses on Feuerbach*, he derives his interest in practice. Weber, perhaps the most important of the trio as an influence, can be seen behind the interest in life-style and status, the extension of market models into fields of analysis other than the economic and the notion of 'the field' as a model for thinking about ongoing social pattern. Durkheim (and indeed, Mauss) is the source of the interest in social classification. These 'canonical' social theorists are, above all, resources to be used as, and if, appropriate:

> . . . one may – and should – use Weber against Weber to go beyond Weber. In the same way, one should follow Marx's advice when he said 'I am not a Marxist', and be an anti-Marxist Marxist. One may think with Weber or Durkheim, or both, against Marx to go beyond Marx and, sometimes, to do what Marx could have done, in his own logic. Each thinker offers the means to transcend the limitation of the others.[27]

Given this 'pragmatic relationship' to other thinkers, it is clear that an 'influence' is as likely to be an author with whom one disagrees as it is someone whose arguments one accepts or is inspired by. In the first sense, Sartre and Lévi-Strauss are both significant influences. In a more positive fashion, and leaving aside Marx, Weber and Durkheim, Bourdieu has clearly been influenced by a diverse range of writers. Two, in particular, strike me as important: Wittgenstein, with his insights into the role of language in the constitution of the social world and lived experience, and Goffman, whose personal brand of interactionism seems to underpin much of Bourdieu's thinking on strategising and games-playing. There are others to whom one might wish to refer – Husserl or Nietzsche, for example – but perhaps it is best to stop the intellectual genealogy here, for the work of the man himself is, after all, what interests us.

And how, before we start, is that work to be summarised? His own most recent characterisation is to describe his project as 'genetic structuralism',[28] the attempt to understand how 'objective', supra-individual social reality (cultural and institutional social structure) and the internalised 'subjective' mental worlds of individuals as cultural beings and social actors are inextricably bound up together, each being a contributor to –

and, indeed, an aspect of – the other. This is Bourdieu's place in the debate on structure and agency.

Another way of looking at Bourdieu's work is to return to his roots as a philosopher. Looked at from that perspective, his research activity is 'fieldwork in philosophy',[29] something to which I have already implicitly alluded earlier in this chapter. But perhaps the fairest way to conclude this section is to allow Bourdieu himself to tell us what it is that he is trying to understand:

> The object of social science is a reality that encompasses all the individual and collective struggles aimed at conserving or transforming reality, in particular those that seek to impose the legitimate definition of reality, whose specifically symbolic efficacy can help to conserve or subvert the established order, that is to say, reality.[30]

READING THIS BOOK

The chapters which follow attempt to trace a logical path through Bourdieu's considerable body of published work. Given his propensity to work and re-work themes in different empirical research contexts, and his enthusiasm for returning to earlier bodies of material in order to further his philosophical fieldwork of the moment, this involves doing a certain amount of violence to his intellectual career. It is to be hoped that the injuries thereby inflicted will only be minor.

Chapter Two focuses upon Bourdieu the social anthropologist and ethnographer and particularly upon his work among the Kabyle in Algeria. Here I will discuss in some detail the importance of structuralism in helping to develop his approach to culture. The subsequent chapter, largely concerned with epistemology and method, is also rooted in his experiences as an ethnographer, of his own and other societies. Epistemology – a critical concern with how and if it is possible to know the world and how one can justify any particular claim to knowledge – is a topic which many people find intimidating. One of the objectives of this chapter will be to make it less so. The main topic will be Bourdieu's view of the need for the social researcher to avoid a misleading reification or objectification of the social reality under study. This is to be achieved, he suggests, by means of an epistemological break, not only with that reality, but also with the research process which produces an account of that reality. Attention will be paid to the role of language use in this 'double distancing' later on, in Chapter Seven.

Chapter Four, on Bourdieu's theories of social practice, perhaps the heart of his work, will argue that, despite his best efforts to transcend the dualistic divide between 'objectivism' and 'subjectivism', his model of humanity, his philosophical anthropology, remains caught in an unresolved contradiction between determinism and voluntarism, with the balance of his argument favouring the former. Chapter Five examines the application of this theoretical framework to the study of the French education system. Bourdieu's reception by the Anglophone sociology of education will also be discussed.

Culture and social hierarchy are the subject matter of Chapter Six. Culture, in Bourdieu's model, is something over and with which status categories fight in the reproduction of the social pecking order. This leads on, in the next chapter, to a discussion of language, power and social distinction, specifically the manner in which language is used by academics in their struggles for professional distinction. Part of this discussion will question the degree to which Bourdieu's *own* use of language is occasioned by the complexity of the issues and topics with which he is dealing, or whether it should, in fact, be viewed as a dimension of the author's own struggle for cultural distinction within a specifically Parisian intellectual context. Finally, in the concluding chapter, I will suggest some ways in which Bourdieu's work can contribute to the further development of social theory and research strategies.

Two other things ought to be said. First, I have no ambition here to even attempt to cover systematically the secondary literature on Bourdieu. There is no space and it has to some extent been done elsewhere.[31] Second, I have confined myself to Bourdieu's major published works in English. This is because my own French is sufficiently limited to make texts of the complexity of Bourdieu's a nightmare to read; because the bulk of his important work is now available in translation; and because an undergraduate audience is unlikely to want to turn to the originals, whereas they might easily be persuaded, as a beginning, to make the effort with, say, *Algeria 1960* or *In Other Words*. The bibliography at the end includes a suggested reading plan for those who are sufficiently interested in Bourdieu's work to get to grips with it at first hand. Although not an easy task, it should prove to be worthwhile, as the rest of this book will attempt to demonstrate.

NOTES AND REFERENCES

[1] P. Bourdieu, *Homo Academicus*, Cambridge, Polity (1988), p. 149.
[2] P. Bourdieu, '*Vive la crise*! For heterodoxy in social science', *Theory and Society*, vol. 17 (1988), pp. 774–5.
[3] P. Bourdieu, *In Other Words: Essays Towards a Reflexive Sociology*, Cambridge, Polity (1990).
[4] See, for example: R. Harker, C. Mahar and C. Wilkes (eds), *An Introduction to the Work of Pierre Bourdieu: The Practice of Theory*, London, Macmillan (1990); D. Robbins, *The Work of Pierre Bourdieu: Recognising Society*, Buckingham, Open University Press (1991).
[5] This is, in fairness, something of which my own critical work has been accused: L.D. Wacquant, 'Towards a Reflexive Sociology: A Workshop with Pierre Bourdieu', *Sociological Theory*, vol. 7 (1989), p. 36.
[6] M. Segalen, 'Current Trends in French Ethnology', *Folk-Life*, vol. 27 (1988–9), p. 11.
[7] M. Bloch, *Ritual, History and Power: Selected Papers in Anthropology*, London, Athlone Press (1989), pp. 117–20.
[8] R. Harker *et al.* (eds), *An Introduction . . .*, *op. cit.*, p. 26.
[9] P. Bourdieu, *In Other Words*, *op. cit.*, p. 4.
[10] A. Honneth, H. Kocyba and B. Schwibs, 'The Struggle for Symbolic Order: An Interview with Pierre Bourdieu', *Theory, Culture and Society*, vol. 3 (1986), p. 44.
[11] P. Bourdieu, *In Other Words*, *op. cit.*, p. 3.
[12] A Honneth *et al.*, 'The Struggle for Symbolic Order', *op. cit.*, pp. 38 and 39.
[13] P. Bourdieu, *The Algerians*, Boston, Beacon Press (1962).
[14] R. Harker *et al.* (eds), *An Introduction . . .*, *op. cit.*, p. 50.
[15] P. Bourdieu, *In Other Words*, *op. cit.*, p. 19.
[16] For discussion of this world, see: T. Clark, *Prophets and Patrons: The French University and the Emergence of the Social Sciences*, Cambridge, Mass., Harvard University Press (1973), and C.C. Lemert (ed.), *French Sociology: Rupture and Renewal since 1968*, New York, Columbia University Press (1981).

[17] P. Bourdieu, *Outline of a Theory of Practice*, Cambridge, Cambridge University Press (1977), p. 74.

[18] P. Bourdieu, *The Logic of Practice*, Cambridge, Polity (1990), p. 9.

[19] P. Bourdieu, *Algeria 1960*, Cambridge, Cambridge University Press (1979), pp. 133–53; also in *The Logic of Practice*, *op. cit.*, pp. 271–83.

[20] A. Honneth *et al.*, 'The Struggle for Symbolic Order', *op. cit.*, p. 41.

[21] P. Bourdieu, *In Other Words*, *op. cit.*, p. 31.

[22] S. Hall, 'The Hinterland of Science: Ideology and the "Sociology of Knowledge" ', in Centre for Contemporary Cultural Studies, *On Ideology*, London, Hutchinson (1978), p. 29.

[23] E.P. Thompson, *The Poverty of Theory*, London, Merlin (1978), p. 366.

[24] J. Karabel and A.H. Halsey, 'Educational Research: A Review and an Interpretation', in J. Karabel and A.K. Halsey (eds), *Power and Ideology in Education*, New York, Oxford University Press (1977), p. 33.

[25] P. Bourdieu, *'Vive la crise!'*, *op. cit.*, p. 780.

[26] P. Bourdieu, *In Other Words*, *op. cit.*, p. 27.

[27] P. Bourdieu, *'Vive la crise!'*, *op. cit.*, p. 780.

[28] P. Bourdieu, *In Other Words*, *op. cit.*, p. 14.

[29] *Ibid*, p. 28.

[30] P. Bourdieu, *The Logic of Practice*, *op. cit.*, p. 141.

[31] See, for example, the bibliographies in: R. Harker *et al.*, *An Introduction . . .*, *op. cit.*, and L.D. Wacquant, 'Towards a Reflexive Sociology', *op. cit.*.

2
Anthropology and Structuralism

Bourdieu arrived in Algeria in 1956 as a soldier and a philosopher; he left in 1960 as a self-taught ethnographer and social anthropologist. He had published his first book and undertaken, in person and using research assistants, field research among the Kabyle peasantry of the Mahgreb and among the urban poor in Algiers and elsewhere. The body of data and ethnography thus accumulated was to provide him with enough material for a substantial body of published work over the subsequent decades. It is something to which, even yet, he still returns on occasions.

As a body of work, however, much of it is not particularly germane to this discussion. *Sociologie de L'Algérie*,[1] in particular, the first book referred to above, is primarily a compendium of information about the various ethnic groups which constituted Algerian society in the 1950s (although towards the end he does begin to say some more interesting things about the effects of war and the nature of the Algerian revolution). The two other collaborative early books on Algeria, about the Algerian working class, published in 1963,[2] and about the crisis in traditional Algerian agriculture, published a year later,[3] are, by and large, similarly prosaic. For much of their length they are almost irrel-

evant to a consideration of the subsequent development of Bourdieu's thinking. [4] The material discussed in the next section –
drawn from articles and from *Algeria 1960* – derives from those
parts of these early works which are analytical rather than
descriptive (and authored by Bourdieu).

Algeria itself is not, however, irrelevant. As an initial experience of ethnographic fieldwork, it was clearly formative with
respect to Bourdieu's epistemological critique of the research
process, something which will be discussed in detail in Chapter
Three. In this chapter, however, I intend to focus on two other
aspects of Bourdieu's Algerian studies which form part of the
mainstream of his intellectual career: first, his analysis of the
relationship between the experience of modernisation (an
unhappy word, but perhaps the most appropriate) and the view
of the world held by Algerian peasants and proletarians, and
second, his structuralist interpretations of Kabyle culture. These
are the subject matter of the first two sections of this chapter.
Following this there will be a discussion of the continuing influence of structuralism on Bourdieu's thought and, finally, I will
talk briefly about his later ethnographic research among the Béarnais peasantry in France, paying particular attention to what he
has described as the theoretical move from 'rules to strategies'.

TIME AND THE DISENCHANTMENT OF THE WORLD

One of the central themes which unifies Bourdieu's work is the
attempt to understand the relationship between 'subjectivity' –
individual social being as it is experienced and lived, from the
personal inside out, so to speak – and the 'objective' social
world within which it is framed and towards the production and
reproduction of which it contributes. This theoretical project is
a key aspect of Bourdieu's attempt to develop a sociology which
can transcend the subjectivist/objectivist dichotomy, as discussed
in Chapter One. It lies at the heart of his notion of genetic
structuralism:

> . . . the analysis of objective structures . . . is inseparable
> from the analysis of the genesis, within biological indi-
> viduals, of the mental structures which are to some
> extent the product of the incorporation of social struc-
> tures; inseparable, too, from the analysis of the genesis
> of these social structures themselves . . .[5]

Perhaps the earliest empirical context from which some of the ideas central to this position can be seen to emerge in Bourdieu's work is the Algerian peasant and urban (sub)proletarian experience of 'development': 'the process by which dispositions and ideologies are adapted to imported and imposed economic structures, i.e. the reinvention of a new system of dispositions under the pressure of economic necessity'.[6] Leaving aside for the moment the throwaway sophistry of the *re*invention of a *new* system – this is the kind of illusory profundity which can make Bourdieu's work so irritating to read – let us focus on his analysis of the Algerian experience of time and, in particular, the orientation to the future.

In a well-known paper, first published in 1963,[7] Bourdieu discusses 'The attitude of the Algerian peasant towards time'. His starting point is that the notion of the future as a 'broad field of innumerable possibilities which man is able to explore and dominate'[8] is one which is alien to indigenous Algerian culture. To say this, however, is not to suggest that the *fellaheen* live in a present which is nothing more than immediacy, divorced from a future which is any further away than an easily imaginable tomorrow. Their experience of time, their conception of the future, is part and parcel of a total relation to the natural world, and particularly the productive earth, in which the Kabyle peasantry submit to, and are part of, the 'vagaries and vigours' of the land and the seasons:

> Submission to nature is inseparable from submission to the passage of time . . . Time stretches out, given a rhythm by the round of work and holidays and by the succession of nights and days. Time so marked is not, as has often been shown, measured time. The intervals of subjective experience are not equal and uniform . . . The 'forthcoming' is perceived in the same manner as the actual present to which it is tied by an organic unity. Potentialities, as distinct from possibilities, are not apprehended as arising from an infinite number of possibilities equally able to come about or not, but as being incapable of not coming about, since, as they are grasped, they are just as much present as the actual present, directly perceived.[9]

The experience of time is, therefore, rooted in and tied to the agricultural world and its 'natural' cycle. The past, the present and the future form part of a continuing and repetitive world of experience which is 'incapable of not coming about'. The cycle of life is one of social reproduction in the continuous medium term.

This is an understanding of the pre-capitalist experience of time which is familiar from the work of E.P. Thompson and others.[10] From this perspective time can be neither wasted nor saved; the basis for Weberian rational calculation does not exist in what is still, in its essence, an enchanted world. Inasmuch as the future is implicit in the past, time, in a sense, stands still.

In another paper, published a year earlier,[11] Bourdieu considers those for whom the spell has been shattered, the Algerian sub-proletariat: 'Entrance into the money economy is coupled with the discovery of time as something that can be wasted, that is, the distinction between empty, or lost, time, or well-filled time'.[12] It is not just the money economy, however. The move from the country to the city also involves exchanging the relative (and modest) security of a peasant way of life in which there is a productive niche – of whatever kind – for everyone, for the impersonal arbitration of the labour market. Work becomes employment, which is a scarce resource. For the first time, perhaps, it becomes *really* possible to have nothing to do. Not only does time spent consciously unemployed become time wasted, but it prevents rational calculation – the epitome of the capitalist world in which the migrant now exists – about the future. The result is 'an obsession with the morrow, a fascination with the immediate'.[13] What is more:

> . . . those who are *in* the condition of the subproletariat cannot comprehend it, since to do so would presuppose their ability to plan an escape. Because it is impossible not to take it as it is, the dream of escaping only means experiencing the weight of necessity more cruelly.[14]

Here we have the beginnings of a set of ideas which Bourdieu was to develop further in a number of settings during the 1960s: a concern with the relationship between 'subjective hopes' and 'objective chances'. First published in French in 1977, *Algeria 1960*,[15] and particularly the long essay entitled 'The Disenchantment of the World' which forms the greater part of the text, represents the apogee of Bourdieu's exploration of this theme in the Algerian context, a reworking of earlier material from 1963's *Travail et traveilleurs en Algérie*. The key idea is that there is an adjustment between the individual's hopes, aspirations, goals and expectations, on the one hand, and the objective situation in which they find themselves by virtue of their place in the social order, on the other. Realism about the future is engendered by the reality of the present:

> Outlooks on the future depend closely on the objective potentialities which are defined for each individual by his or her social status and material conditions of existence. The most individual project is never anything other than an aspect of the subjective expectations that are attached to that agent's class.[16]

What is attempted, therefore, is, by and large, what is possible. The greater the number of things which become or are possible, the more options which one is offered or confronted by, the closer the fit becomes between aspiration and likelihood. As an individual rises up the social hierarchy of status and class, so the vista of the realistically attainable deepens and widens, if only in small degree. Choices and projects, conceived within and conditioned by an enhanced freedom of action, become evermore – and somewhat paradoxically perhaps – framed within a conservative opting for what can be done. A plateau of security is reached, where life ceases to be the desperate mere pursuit of subsistence, and the worker arrives at a 'threshold of calculability' beyond which his or her conduct becomes, in all spheres, even the domestic ('the site of the last resistances'), rationalised with respect to a more or less predictable future.[17]

For the unemployed sub-proletarian, however, the Algerian city offers a different situation. Their poverty 'imposes itself on them with a necessity so total that it allows them no glimpse of a reasonable exit'.[18] They experience their plight as inevitable and natural, something about which they can do nothing. In an analysis which bears more than a passing resemblance to Oscar Lewis's much-criticised notion of the 'culture of poverty',[19] Bourdieu argues that the sub-proletarian experience of economic insecurity and blocked employment opportunities – their objective probability – renders them incapable of imagining the possibility of social change. Rather than blaming the 'objective order' for their disadvantage, they fall back on their own inadequacies as the explanation for their distress. This, once again, is the 'subjective expectation of objective probabilities'.

It is not merely at the level of the individual that this process operates, however, and it is at the collective level that it acquires a major political significance. Individuals may apprehend not only their personal future, but also the 'objective, collective future' of the social category to which they belong and the possibilities which it offers. For the reasons discussed immediately above it is the working proletariat, those who occupy a precarious plateau of economic security, not the sub-proletariat, who may begin to conceive of an alternative future, as a consequence of their 'open and rational temporal consciousness'. Bourdieu's argument at this point, concerning the revolutionary potential of the Algerian sub-proletariat (or, more exactly, its absence), is explicitly intended by him as a refutation of the writings of Frantz Fanon on the Algerian revolution and 'third world' liberation struggles.[20] Here, perhaps, we can also pick up an echo of Marx's distinction between 'a class in itself' and 'a class for itself', or even of Lenin's argument that revolution is not an inevitable result of the emiseration and oppression of the working class:

> The effort to master the future cannot be undertaken in reality until the conditions indispensable for ensuring it a minimum chance of success are actually provided. Until this is the case, the only possible attitude is forced traditionalism, which differs essentially from adherence to tradition, because it implies the possibility of acting differently and the impossibility of enacting that possibility.[21]

This, for the moment, is where we will leave it. Bourdieu's model of the relationship between 'subjective expectations' and 'objective probabilities' is vulnerable to a number of criticisms – of circularity, determinism and materialism, in particular – which will be explored in detail in Chapters Four and Five. Suffice it that the roots of the notion in his Algerian experience have been adequately established.

His discussion of the 'disenchantment of the world' experienced by migrants from the Algerian countryside to the town closes with an analysis of modern housing as an impoverishing and, paradoxically, constraining domestic environment. It is a concrete representation of a future which cannot be, yet demands to be, achieved. It is to a more celebrated and widely read analysis of domestic space and architecture – 'The Kabyle house or the world reversed' – that our discussion will now turn.

'BLISSFUL STRUCTURALISM': THE BERBER HOUSE

Perhaps the best place to start is with structuralism itself: what was Bourdieu embracing so enthusiastically in the early 1960s and what was it against which he appears to have reacted so strongly subsequently? To ask these questions, however, is easier than to answer them. There is, in an important sense, no such thing as 'structuralism'. There are, rather, a variety of structuralist approaches to culture and social reality[22]: Piaget, Lévi-Strauss, Althusser, Chomsky, Foucault and Leach – not to mention Bourdieu himself – have all been described, by themselves or others, at some time or another, as 'structuralists'.

The intellectual thread which may serve to unite this disparate ensemble goes back to the work of the Swiss linguist Saussure in the early years of the twentieth century. For our purposes, two aspects of Saussure's work are important. First, his distinction between the grammatical or logical structure of language (*langue*) and the everyday, improvisational hurly-burly of speech (*parole*), together with his insistence that the former is the appropriate domain for the location and analysis of meaning, laid the foundation for the structuralist method: the true nature of social phenomena as relational systems of meaning is to be sought in structure, which lies somehow behind or beneath the phenomenal world of appearances. Second, he argued that aspects of culture or social life other than language could also be treated as systems for the signification of meaning, each with an appropriate structure or structures to be revealed or deciphered.

With respect to the first of these, Saussure clearly stands in a broad epistemological tradition of realism – including such diverse thinkers as Marx and Freud – which starts off from the position that things social are rarely, if ever, as they seem. Their reality or essence must be discovered beneath the surface world of what people do and say in social interaction. In the second, Saussure was establishing the basis for a burgeoning new tradition of cultural analysis, a tradition in which universes of meaning could be discovered everywhere from dining-table place settings to wrestling matches. The mundane world becomes transformed into a pregnant network of signification and communication, awaiting only the midwife's touch of the analyst for the message(s) to be delivered.

Linguistics also supplied the other important component of structuralism, in the ideas of Jakobson from the 1920s and 1930s.

Meaning, for Jakobson as for Saussure, is arbitrary and socially defined: there is no necessary connection between signifier and signified. However, he identified, in his analysis of language, what has come to be seen as *the* elementary structure of meaning by many subsequent structuralists, binary opposition. The hierarchical and dualistic contrast of like with unlike is regarded as the key to hidden semantic structure, in language and in culture generally. In the work of Lévi-Strauss, particularly his studies of myth, this is interpreted as revealing a fundamental aspect of the way in which the human mind functions. Binary opposition is one of the brain's most basic operations; it is a deep and primeval structuring principle of culture.

Without wishing to anticipate later arguments, there are a number of related criticisms of the structuralist approach which are relevant here. First, as a synchronic method, concerned to identify or construct models of invariate or slowly transforming structure, structuralism precludes diachronic or historical analysis. It is a quest for law-like systemic or relational properties – binary oppositions, for example – rather than an attempt to understand social process over time. Second, the details of what people say or do, and how they say or do it – the ins and outs of social interaction – are, at best, of limited interest to structuralism, either as data contributing to explanation or as something to be explained. Third, given that structural truth lies hidden behind the mask of everyday life, structuralism – much as psychoanalysis – is vulnerable to accusations that it only finds what it looks for. In this sense structure may, as with beauty, lie in the eye of the beholder. Like psychoanalysis, structuralism has to posit the existence of an unconscious domain of affect and cognition, interpretable and detectable only through its reflection in the expressive forms which are assumed to be its product.

Bourdieu's relationship with structuralism during the 1960s is not easy to reconstruct. The previous section has, for example, shown us a side to his Algerian studies which is very *un*-structuralist. What is more:

> I can state without exaggeration that I resisted with all my strength the trendy forms of structuralism – which seem at times to be the only ones that were received abroad – when I tried to introduce structural, or relational, ideas into sociology. I also found the

mechanistic application of Saussure and Jakobson unacceptable . . .[23]

On the other hand, however, there is his own characterisation of himself as a 'blissful structuralist'.[24] This bliss found its strongest and most effective expression in his exegesis of the symbolism embodied in the domestic space of the Berber (or Kabyle) house,[25] written in 1963 but first published in 1970 in a volume celebrating Lévi-Strauss's sixtieth birthday. This was an appropriate context for a most impressive *tour de force* of structuralist analysis.

The Kabyle house is rectangular, typically divided into two distinct parts by an internal half-wall: one-third is stable space, the rest is for humans and is higher than the animal's area. A large front door in the eastern long wall allows entrance to both rooms, a smaller back door in the western wall is for humans only. The front door is for men, the back door for women. Entering from the east by the front door, the hearth and the cooking area are on one's right, at the opposite end of the house from the stable. A weaving loom faces the front door, against the west wall by the back door. The half-wall to the left of the front door is where dried vegetables and figs are kept; it is also where the man of the house sleeps and where his wife from time to time joins him from her usual bed in the stable. Grain is stored by the north wall, on either side of the cooking area, and water by the front door.

To describe it thus, even to draw a plan,[26] one does not begin to say anything meaningful about the house from a structuralist point of view. As a microcosm of an entire cultural world, it is a condensed universe full of meaning. From its organisation, the social relations between its contents and parts, can be read off the principles which are the supporting generative framework of Kabyle culture and cosmology.

The key to the house's complex code is to be found, in the first place, in the binary oppositions which it embodies. The most obvious of these are inside and outside, east and west (the building is normally oriented with its long axis on a north–south line) and back and front. Passing inside – from the public world of men to the private domain of women – one confronts a host of competing oppositional couplets, some of which are more self-evident than others. The contrast between the light, dry, upper, human part of the house, on the one hand, and the dark, damp, lower, animal quarters, on the other, (which is simultaneously one opposition and many) is perhaps the most easily envisaged. There are, however, many others: fire and water; the weaving-loom wall and the door wall; the (male) master beam of the house, supporting the roof, and the main (female) pillar upon which it rests; grain for consumption and grain for sowing; and so on.

These concrete, material oppositions are not all there is to it, however. Abstract conceptual opposition is also tied in to the system: the cooked and the raw, that which is fertilising and that which is able to be fertilised, *nif* (male honour) and *hurma* (female honour), day and night; there is a multitude of such notions. The point is, of course, that the concrete and the abstract are systematically related in a manner which is not simply 'given' by the nature or function of the artifacts concerned: '. . . these oppositions [i.e. between material objects] are the centre of a cluster of parallel oppositions the necessity of which never stems entirely from technical imperatives and functional requirements . . .'[27] Thus the tangible presence of artifacts, commodities and physical structures symbolises and refers to the abstract cultural order of values and interpretive morality. A partial list of equivalences might look something like this:

Male	:	Female
outside	:	inside
high	:	low
light	:	dark
cooked	:	raw
grain for eating	:	grain for saving
that which is fertilising	:	that which can be fertilised
weaving-loom wall	:	door wall
nif	:	*hurma*

Such a list might be genuinely endless.[28] Suffice that it should make the point that binary oppositions, constructed (by the anthropologist or by the culture?) in this fashion, nestle and interlock in complex ways. Some – male:female, culture:nature, for example – are regarded as basic. As elementary organising principles, they imbue the rest of the system with their character or flavour. All, however, derive their meaning(s) from their oppositional form – one arm making sense of the other – in the first place, and their place in the system as a whole, in the second. For example, while the outside of the house is male and the inside female, the interior (female) is itself structured into upper (male) and lower (female), and so on. Opposition and homology are complementary and hierarchical processes.

Gender lies at the heart of the Kabyle system of classification. It is related, via a maze of oppositional dyads and ritual practices, to the fertility of the fields and the house. However, the relationship between male and female is not egalitarian:

> The orientation of the house is fundamentally defined from outside, from the standpoint of men, and, so to speak, by men and for men, as the place men come out of . . . One must not be misled by the appearance of symmetry . . .[29]

Herein lies the explanation of Bourdieu's sub-title for this piece, 'the world reversed'. The east is the sunrise, birth, prosperity – it is a male orientation. The man comes from the east to enter the house via the front door in the eastern wall. However, the internal symbolic geography of the house reverses the external order of things: the inside of the (western) weaving-loom wall, which he meets and upon which the light of the sunrise falls through the open door, is classified as 'the east of the inside'. The inside face of the eastern wall is, correspondingly, 'the west of the house'. With respect to the organisation of internal domestic space, 'its orientation is exactly the reverse of that of external space'.[30] All of which means that, whether going in or coming out, crossing the threshold which is the magical pivot of the system, the man faces east: 'one is able both to go in and out on the right foot, literally and figuratively . . . one enters it facing the light and also comes out of it facing the light'.[31]

It is not possible to do justice here to the ethnographic and imaginative richness of Bourdieu's analysis; read it. When you have finished you will probably want to read it again. Not for nothing does it seem to be one of his own favourite pieces. It is, of course, open to the criticisms of the structuralist method suggested earlier. There is no sense, for example, of anything other than a timeless ethnographic present. Insofar as what people say or do enters into the picture at all, it is usually either as proscriptive rules – 'it is forbidden to . . .' or 'a woman must never . . .' – or stylised, proverbial aphorisms. Consequently, despite this ethnography, it is not clear whether the symbolic edifice of binary oppositions exists in some sense in the culture and discourse of the Kabyle people, or whether it has simply been imposed by the anthropologist, who is thus its creator.

However, 'The Kabyle house' should not be dismissed as *just* structuralism, albeit a superb example of the genre. In one important sense, 'the attention given to the movements and displacements of the body',[32] Bourdieu in this paper, written let us remember in 1963, prefigures his own later development of the concept of the habitus and his subsequent analyses of the logic of practice. It is from the point of view of a (male) *embodied* Berber peasant that the spatial rotation of the internal and external universes is identified and made to make sense. What is more, adopting this analytical standpoint began to make clear to him the limitations of structuralism:

> . . . to account for the quasi-miraculous and therefore somewhat incredible necessity, without any organizing intention, that was revealed by analysis, one had to look at the incorporated dispositions, or more precisely the body schema, to find the ordering principle . . . capable of orienting practices in a way that is at once unconscious and systematic. [33]

Structuralism may have been a stimulating intellectual game, but it did not contribute much to Bourdieu's attempt to understand how things get done, how a particular set of practices is experienced 'without any organizing intention' as necessary: 'how x must be done', 'there is nothing else to be done' or whatever.

Structuralism was of enormous importance, however, because it made his difficulty and his intellectual project clear. The more structuralism seeks to impose system and coherence on the practice of men and women and its products, the more the limits of the systematicity and coherence of both practice and products becomes apparent. Particularly in the use of the diagrammatic schemes – of seasonal cycles, domestic space, cooking cycles, etc. – which analyses of this kind encourage, he found himself increasingly imposing upon his ethnographic material a synchronised and comprehensive order which, paradoxically perhaps, increasingly revealed itself as false and inadequate.[34] This problem, which Bourdieu has called the 'synoptic illusion', will be explored in the next chapter.

FURTHER EXPLORATIONS OF SYMBOLISM AND CLASSIFICATION

It is clear that Bourdieu's Kabyle ethnography exerts an abiding fascination over his imagination. Apart from *Algeria 1960*, he has drawn extensively upon this material in *Outline of a Theory of Practice* and its successor, *The Logic of Practice*. It is also clear that, despite his protestations, some elements of a structuralist approach to culture remain important in his thinking. This becomes most apparent in the long chapter on 'Irresistible Analogy' which (apart from yet another appearance of 'The Kabyle house', this time as an appendix) serves to close *Logic*.

While rejecting both the reification or over-ordering of culture produced by structuralism and the objectification of social reality which results from the epistemological naivety of conventional ethnography, Bourdieu recognises that there is order and pattern in the system of dispositions and schemes which he refers to as the habitus (and which we, for the moment, will equate with 'culture'; it will be discussed further in Chapter Four). It is not *all* in the eye of the beholder. The 'reality' of cultural structure can, according to Bourdieu, be grasped by means of four basic propositions.

First, to see the world – in the cultural rather than the optical sense, in other words to have a world-view – is to categorise or classify the world. Second, classification is based on an archetypal binary or dualistic model of order:

> A vision of the world is a division of the world, based on a fundamental principle of division which distributes all the things of the world to the complementary classes. To bring order is to bring division, to divide the universe into opposing entities . . . The limit produces difference and the different things 'by an arbitrary institution' . . . This magical act presupposes and produces collective belief, that is, ignorance of its own arbitrariness . . . the group constitutes itself as such by instituting what unites and what separates it. The cultural act *par excellence* is the one that traces the line that produces a separate, delimited space . . .[35]

The debt to structuralism is obvious. Binary opposition is *the* universal or elementary classificatory principle. It does not, however, have its origins in neurology or cognitive process. This is the third point. The fundamental binary division, and the model for all others, is that of gender: 'The limit *par excellence*, that between the sexes, will not brook transgression. . .'.[36] It is located as much in the real world as anywhere else. Finally, this elementary division provides the sub-text, through processes of analogy (and, he might also have said, homology) for all the other binary classifications of the system, and, indeed, of *all* systems. It is the basic generative separation which provides the model and the interpretive paradigm or key for all other classificatory acts of separation and division.

It can only do this, however, because, as with men and women, the distinctions which provide the basis for making distinctions – which are in part constructed by analogy with gender and, by further analogy, illuminate other classificatory oppositions – are in some sense *real*. Up and down, back and front, left and right, hot and cold, for example, are all sensible from the point of view of the embodied person: they are 'logical and biological', 'bodily dispositions' which make sense out of and because of sensation. They are both real (natural) *and* arbitrary (cultural). So, of course, is sex/gender. What Bourdieu is doing to Lévi-Straussian structural analysis here is analogous to what Marx did to Hegelian idealism when he appropriated the dialectic and turned it right side up (or upside down, depending on your point of view). The result is a basically materialist reading of symbolism and classification, in which culture is rooted in the necessary physical embodiment(s) of its producers, women and men.

Magic and ritual are also, it is clear, rooted in the same soil. All magic and all ritual/symbolic practices are, it seems, explicable in terms of 'two operational schemes' which are 'natural processes culturally constituted in and through ritual practice'.[37] The first operation is the reunification of the opposite sides of a classificatory divide; examples here are marriage or the quenching of hot iron (fire) in water. The second is, of course, the reverse: the separation of opposites which have been previously ritually united (an example of which is harvesting, the crop being the product of the fecund combination of various male and female principles and activities). The fundamental division is magical and symbolically loaded, as are its analogies.

In creating this vision of symbolic order, Bourdieu has gone some way beyond structuralism. There remain, however, some of the same problems: it is a synchronic, ahistorical view of the world in which, despite the importance of the body as an organising

metaphor and material point of reference, the day-to-day practices of real men and women seem somewhat remote and determined. Although he attempts to ground his classificatory scheme
in the material, real world of the (culturally constituted) body
and its dispositions, how much of what Bourdieu shows us is
actually 'out there' and how much his own creation remains a
moot point. In addition, there is a further difficulty, although it
is of a different order: the relationship between nature and culture as he outlines it, the relationship between the real and the
arbitrary, is, at best, imprecise, and, at worst, contradictory.

This is not accidental nor is it necessarily a problem. Bourdieu
is attempting to communicate something here of the complexity
of a natural world with cultural people in it. It is also part of
his attempt to overcome the division between objectivism and
subjectivism which in his view bedevils social science. It requires
creative effort on the part of his audience, if they are to follow
the argument. Whether or not, having followed it, it is intelligible
is, perhaps, the best indicator of the strength of the objectivist/
subjectivist dualism that Bourdieu himself could wish for.

The important point, however, is that the vagueness is as much
a part of the social processes and situations which Bourdieu is
attempting to understand as it is part of his argument:

> Our perception and our practice, especially our percep-
> tion of the social world, are guided by practical taxo-
> nomies, oppositions between up and down, masculine
> (or virile) and feminine, etc., and the classifications pro-
> duced by these taxonomies owe their effectiveness to
> the fact that they are 'practical', that they allow one to
> introduce just enough logic for the needs of practical
> behaviour, neither too much – since a certain vagueness
> is often indispensable, especially in negotiations – nor
> too little, since life would then be impossible.[38]

These 'practical taxonomies' linked by processes of generative
analogy and homology, are important to Bourdieu's model of
practice. It is to another important element of that model, the
notion of strategising, that we will now turn our attention.

FROM RULES TO STRATEGIES

As we saw in the previous chapter, one of the reasons for Bourdieu's theoretical move beyond structuralism was his dissatis-

faction with its lack of predictive power. The rules which structuralist analyses – whether of a weak or strong variety – generate do not seem to explain very much when it comes to what people actually do:

> . . . I was surprised to find, on the basis of statistical material – which is employed relatively rarely in ethnology, that the supposedly predominant type of marriage in Algerian-Berber societies, i.e. marriage to a parallel cousin, accounts for only 3 to 4% of all cases, and 5 to 6% in the strict, orthodox families of the Marabu. This led me to consider in more depth such concepts as 'kinship', 'kinship regulation', 'rule', and led finally to results that contradicted the structuralist tradition.[39]

The realisation that the generalisations about behaviour – marriage rules, ritual procedures or whatever – produced by anthropology, particularly structuralist anthropology, were often neither predictive nor descriptive led Bourdieu in two directions. In the first, he developed his epistemological critique of research practice and sociological knowledge (this will be the focus of the next chapter). In the second, he replaced the notion of rules which govern or produce conduct with a model of social practice in which what people do is bound up with the generation and pursuit of strategies within an organising framework of cultural dispositions (the habitus). This will be the main subject for discussion in Chapter Four. We will look at the issue in brief here because it seems to have arisen, in the first instance, from his experience as an ethnographer.

As the quotation immediately above makes clear, it was the marriage patterns of the Berber peasantry of Algeria which first alerted Bourdieu to the contours and dimensions of the problem.[40] Here he was particularly concerned with the distinction between the official version – the ideology, who *ought* to marry whom, the *rule* – and practical kinship, who *actually* married whom and the familial strategies which brought these outcomes about. The official ideology of marriage preference – for the patrilateral parallel cousin – is, in fact, a rhetorical resource, to be drawn upon or not as circumstances require; it is emphatically not a proscription.

The contradiction between anthropological accounts and statistical accounts led Bourdieu to scepticism about preferential marriage rules. In another area of his Algerian studies – his analysis of the Kabyle sense of honour, first published in 1965[41] – it seems to have been a more conventional engagement with ethnography which led him to look at strategising. In the game of 'challenge and riposte' which is the ongoing process of the maintenance, accumulation or loss of public honour in (male) Kabyle society, honour-related behaviours are not rule-governed. Rather, there is a diffuse and generalised 'sense of honour', learned and nurtured since childhood, which, in the context of the dispositions and practical taxonomies of Kabyle culture, produces the logic of transactions between men and families. The 'sense of honour' only makes sense, what is more, when chains of transactions are viewed over time: interval, pause and timing are crucial elements in the improvisatory practice that is the foundation of interactional competence. Honour, then, in Kabyle society, does not appear to be a fixed or definite value, equivalent perhaps to a jurally-defined status. It is, Bourdieu suggests, best understood as, for each individual or family, an ongoing practical accomplishment, socially constructed in the to-ing and fro-ing of transaction and exchange. As an aside, it is worth pointing out that Bourdieu's interest in the sense of honour among the Kabyle is the precursor of a long-standing interest in struggles for social recognition and the pursuit of symbolic capital.[42]

Bourdieu's final experience of 'real anthropology' appears to have been his fieldwork among the small farmers of the Béarn, in south-western France, in 1960.[43] Here, in the area where he had spent his childhood, he came face to face with the inadequacy of formalistic models of social structure. Once again, the substantive context was provided by marriage patterns and strategies, particularly as they related to land and inheritance. In the context of this analysis, he found himself adopting a vocabulary of 'matrimonial strategies' and 'the social uses of kinship', rather than 'kinship rules', in an attempt to avoid attributing behaviour to the sociological theories which are developed to account for or explain it.[44] Further, he became concerned about the semantic ambiguity of the word 'rule': does it mean (a) a principle governing behaviour which is understood and produced by actors themselves, (b) the 'objective' constraints that govern behaviour in any particular social context, or (c) the explanatory model(s) of the social scientist? These three regularly become confused, (c) often being passed off as (a) or (b) to the detriment of analytical clarity.

Looking at the Béarn ethnography, we can discern many similarities with the Algerian studies of marriage and honour. There appeared to be formal, official rules dictating how family property should be divided up among children: primogeniture – inheritance of the land by the eldest son – prevailed, with younger sons and daughters entitled to compensation for their renunciation of claim to the land in the form of a specific share of the patrimony on marriage. In fact, such a 'rule', observed in strict fact, would have led to the division and break-up of land holdings. In practice:

> The head of the family was in fact always at liberty to manipulate the 'rules' . . . All means were justified when it came to protecting the integrity of the patrimony and preventing the potential division of the estate and the family which every marriage could threaten to bring about.[45]

As with Kabyle honour-related transactions, the pattern only made sense over time: each marriage, and the transactional manoeuvering which it involved, could only be understood in the proper context of an ongoing family strategy aimed at preserving the landholding, and an ongoing series of material and symbolic exchanges between families.

In this chapter Bourdieu's ethnographic work has been discussed in order to demonstrate the roots of much of his subsequent theoretical development in that experience. In particular, his ideas about the subjective expectation of objective probability, the embodiment of culture, practical taxonomies, the competition for symbolic capital and strategising clearly have their origins in this early period of his career. In Chapter Three we will look in more detail at the other major area of his thinking for which this seems also to be true, the epistemological critique of sociological knowledge and research practice.

NOTES AND REFERENCES

[1] P. Bourdieu, *Sociologie de L'Algérie*, Paris, Presses Universitaires de France (1958). English translation: *The Algerians*, Boston, Beacon Press (1962).

[2] P. Bourdieu, and A. Sayad, *Le déracinement: La crise de l'agriculture traditionelle en Algérie*, Paris, Les Éditions de Minuit (1964).

[3] P. Bourdieu, A. Darbel, J.-P. Rivet and C. Siebel, *Travail et travailleurs en Algérie*, Paris, Mouton (1963).

[4] Although stylistically, particularly with their use of statistics, and in their reflection upon method, they are a sign of things to come. For a detailed, and more positive, assessment of these works see D. Robbins, *The Work of Pierre Bourdieu*, Buckingham, Open University Press (1991), pp. 23–8.

[5] P. Bourdieu, *In Other Words: Essays Towards a Reflexive Sociology*, Cambridge, Polity (1990), p. 14.

[6] P. Bourdieu, *Algeria 1960*, Cambridge, Cambridge University Press (1979), p. 5.

[7] P. Bourdieu, 'The Attitude of the Algerian Peasant toward Time', in J. Pitt-Rivers (ed.), *Mediterranean Countrymen*, Paris, Mouton (1963).

[8] *Ibid.*, p. 55.

[9] *Ibid.*, pp. 57, 59, 61–2.

[10] E.P. Thompson, 'Time, Work-Discipline and Industrial Capitalism', *Past and Present*, vol. 38 (1967), pp. 56–97. Thompson refers in this seminal paper to Bourdieu's work on Algerian perceptions of time.

[11] P. Bourdieu, 'The Algerian Subproletariat', in I.W. Zarman (ed.), *Man, State and Society in the Contemporary Mahgreb*, New York, Praeger (1973). Originally published, in French, in *Les Temps Modernes*, no. 199 (1962), pp. 1031–51.

[12] P. Bourdieu, 'Algerian Subproletariat', p. 83.

[13] *Ibid.*, p. 84.

[14] *Ibid.*, p. 91.

[15] P. Bourdieu, *Algeria 1960*, *op. cit.*; French edition, *Algérie 60: structures économiques et structures temporelles*, Paris, Les Éditions de Minuit (1977).

[16] P. Bourdieu, *Algérie 1960*, *op. cit.*, p. 53.

[17] *Ibid.*, p. 54.

[18] *Ibid.*, p. 61.

[19] O. Lewis, 'The Culture of Poverty', *Scientific American*, 215, no. 4 (1966), pp. 19–25. For trenchant criticism of the concept, see: E.B. Leacock (ed.), *The Culture of Poverty: A Critique*, New York, Simon and Schuster (1971), and C.A. Valentine, *Culture and Poverty: Critique and Counter Proposals*, Chicago, University of Chicago Press (1968).

[20] F. Fanon, *The Wretched of the Earth*, Harmondsworth, Penguin (1967), and *A Dying Colonialism*, Harmondsworth, Pelican (1970).

[21] P. Bourdieu, *Algeria 1960*, *op. cit.*, p. 73.

[22] On structuralism see, among others, the following: A. Giddens, 'Structuralism, Post-structuralism and the Production of Culture', in A. Giddens and J. Turner (ed.), *Social Theory Today*, Cambridge, Polity (1987); E. Leach, *Lévi-Strauss*, London, Fontana (1970); E. Leach, *Culture and Communication*, Cambridge, Cambridge University Press (1976); J. Piaget, *Structuralism*, London, Routledge and Kegan Paul (1971); B. Schwartz, *Vertical Classification*, Chicago, University of Chicago Press (1981).

[23] A. Honneth, H. Kocyba and B. Schwibs, 'The Struggle for Symbolic Order: An Interview with Pierre Bourdieu', *Theory, Culture and Society*, vol. 3 no. 3 (1986), p. 38.

[24] P. Bourdieu, *The Logic of Practice*, Cambridge, Polity (1990), p. 9.

[25] P. Bourdieu, 'La maison Kabyle ou le monde renversé', in J. Pouillon and P. Maranda (eds), *Échanges et communications: Melanges offerts à Claude Lévi-Strauss a l'occasion de son 60ème anniversaire*, Paris, Mouton (1970). Various English language versions of this are available: *Social Science Information*, 9 (1970), pp. 151–70; M. Douglas (ed.), *Rules and Meanings*, Harmondsworth, Penguin (1973), pp. 98–110; P. Bourdieu, *Algeria 1960*, *op. cit.*, pp. 133–53; P. Bourdieu, *The Logic of Practice*, *op. cit.*, pp. 271–83. He also draws upon the analysis in *Outline of a Theory of Practice*. It is clearly one of his favourite pieces.

[26] See the diagram of an ideal-typical Berber House: P. Bourdieu, *Algeria 1960*, *op. cit.*, p. 134; P. Bourdieu, *The Logic of Practice*, *op. cit.*, p. 272.

[27] P. Bourdieu, *Algeria 1960*, *op. cit.*, p. 135.

[28] See the synoptic diagrams of Kabyle classificatory schema: P. Bourdieu, *Outline of a Theory of Practice*, Cambridge, Cambridge University Press (1977), p. 157; *Logic of Practice*, *op. cit.*, p. 215.

[29] P. Bourdieu, *Algeria 1960*, *op. cit.*, p. 153.

[30] *Ibid.*, p. 150.

[31] *Ibid.*, p. 152.

[32] P. Bourdieu, *The Logic of Practice*, *op. cit.*, p. 316.

[33] *Ibid.*, p. 10.

[34] *Ibid.*, pp. 10–12, 200–202; P. Bourdieu, *Outline of a Theory. . .*, *op. cit.*, pp. 97–109.

[35] P. Bourdieu, *The Logic of Practice*, *op. cit.*, p. 210.

[36] *Ibid.*, p. 211.

[37] *Ibid.*, p. 223.

[38] P. Bourdieu, *In Other Words*, *op. cit.*, p. 73.

[39] A. Honneth *et al.*, 'The Struggle for Symbolic Order', *op. cit.*, p. 40.

[40] P. Bourdieu, *Outline of a Theory . . .*, *op. cit.*, pp. 30–71; *The Logic of Practice*, *op. cit.*, pp. 162–99.

[41] P. Bourdieu, 'The Sentiment of Honour in Kabyle Society', in J.G. Peristiany (ed.), *Honour and Shame*, London, Weidenfeld and Nicolson (1965). See also: P. Bourdieu, *Outline of a Theory . . .*, *op. cit.*, pp. 10–15; *Algeria 1960*, *op. cit.*, pp. 93–153; *The Logic of Practice*, *op. cit.*, pp. 98–111.

[42] P. Bourdieu, *In Other Words*, *op. cit.*, p. 22.

[43] P. Bourdieu, *The Logic of Practice*, *op. cit.*, pp. 147–61.

[44] P. Bourdieu, *In Other Words*, *op. cit.*, pp. 59–61, for a discussion of these points.

[45] P. Bourdieu, *The Logic of Practice*, *op. cit.*, pp. 150, 151.

3

Experiments in Epistemology

Bourdieu's theoretical shift, from an approach based upon analytical models constructed from the cultural rules supposedly governing behaviour to an emphasis upon the generation and pursuit by actors of strategies, was part of his intellectual and political movement away from structuralism. It was also a response to his experience of doing ethnographic research, first in Algeria and subsequently in France. However, the ethnographic nature of his research experience – fieldwork as a transformative life event – was significant in another respect. His engagement as a social researcher with social worlds with which he was familiar – actually more than familiar, since in each case he was in some sense a legitimate *member* – sparked off the reflexive train of thought leading to his epistemological critique of sociology and anthropology.

Epistemology often seems to hold peculiar terrors for students. This may be because of the manner in which the word is used in social science texts – frequently without definition or explanation – and the remote density of those texts which call themselves epistemological. In fact, at its most basic, epistemology is neither especially complex nor divorced from the mundane concerns of everyday life. Epistemology is the discourse about the nature and status of knowledge.[1] The key questions which it involves are not difficult to understand (although they may prove very difficult to answer): How do I know *x*? How is it possible to say that I know *x*? What is the status or authority of my knowledge of *x*? And so on. These questions are both practical (to do with *method*) and philosophical or theoretical (they form the basis of *methodology*, the discourse about method). Although they are often sharply distinguished, the practical and the philosophical ought not to be seen as separate, nor should one be prioritised over the other.

An even-handed perspective of this kind generates another set of questions: What should I do in order to know *x*? How should I do it? What are the implications for my knowledge of *x* of adopting one research procedure rather than another? It is one of the greatest strengths of Bourdieu's sociology that he has never lost sight of the practicality of epistemological issues (or of their importance).

It is in this context that one must understand Bourdieu's studies of the Béarn district, where he grew up and to which he subsequently returned as an ethnographer, and the institutions of higher education in France, where he trained, worked, struggled for professional recognition and advancement and undertook a protracted kind of participant-observer research. These encounters with his own backyard inspired him to reflect upon the research process and the relative status of 'insider knowledge' and 'outsider knowledge' in sociological accounts and theorising. His subsequent arguments are an interesting inversion of the conventional anthropological wisdom which insists that immersion in the alien or the exotic is a necessary professional *rite de passage* and the basis for the discipline's epistemological authority. Bourdieu's point is that authority and epistemological integrity can best be produced by a reflexive encounter with the 'known', with the apparently familiar:

> *Homo Academicus* represents the culmination, at least in a biographical sense, of a very self-conscious 'epistemological experiment' I started in the early 1960s when I set out to apply to my most familiar universe the methods of investigation I had previously used to uncover the logic of kinship relations in a foreign universe, that of Algerian peasants and subproletarians.

The 'methodological' intent of this research, if we may call it that, was to overturn the natural relation of the observer to his universe of study, to make the mundane exotic and the exotic mundane, in order to render explicit what, in both cases, is taken for granted and to offer a very concrete, very pragmatic, vindication of the possibility of a full sociological objectivation of the object *and* of the subject's relation to the object – what I call *participant objectivation*.[2]

These epistemological issues and problems lie at the heart of Bourdieu's sociological project. Although they represent, in my view, the major part of any claim which Bourdieu has to either originality or heavyweight intellectual significance, they have been but little discussed in the critical literature which his work has generated.[3] Since the beginning is usually the best place to start anything, I will turn first to the notion of participant objectivation.

THE RETURN OF THE NATIVE

What, then, of Bourdieu's epistemological experiment? What was he trying to do? It was an attempt to observe a given social situation from an analytical or sociological point of view and *also* to scrutinise both the 'scientific' stance *vis-à-vis* that situation and the effect of adopting such a stance upon the resultant sociological knowledge of that situation. Thus, the first step back is from the situation in question – this is one of the usual senses in which we talk about 'objectivity' – while the second step back is from the act of observation itself.[4] This, in Bourdieu's words, results in the 'objectification of the act of objectification'; this is necessary because, without so doing, it is impossible to appreciate the nature of most sociological and anthropological accounts of social life.

And what precisely, in Bourdieu's view, is the nature of these accounts? They are, in the first instance, remote or distant accounts. They are superior, insofar as they purport to offer an account of 'what's really going on'. They are more 'knowing', certainly they claim to be more knowledgeable and authoritative, than native interpretations. They adopt a 'theoretical posture' to the social world in question: their aim lies, strictly speaking, outside that world and in that sense they are non-practical.

Sociological knowledge, then, is divorced from the knowledge required to *do* the things about which sociology purports to know. Further, Bourdieu is suggesting that the act of observation, in itself, produces a particular kind of understanding:

> Social science must not only, as objectivism would have it, break with native experience and the native representation of that experience, but also, by a second break, call into question the presuppositions inherent in the position of the 'objective' observer who, seeking to interpret practices, tends to bring into the object the principles of his relation to the object, as is shown for example by the privileged status he gives to communicative and epistemic functions, which inclines him to reduce exchanges to pure symbolic exchanges.[5]

In other words, the point of view of the detached sociological observer – looking for explanations – produces a distorted understanding of the situation in question, a view which reifies and overemphasises ideals, norms, values, etc. These become represented as the 'rules' which govern or determine social action. Bourdieu's epistemological critique is, therefore, inextricably bound up with his theoretical move 'from rules to strategies'. The model of social behaviour as rule-governed is a product, at least in part, of the objectification inherent in looking at social life at one remove:

> in taking up a point of view on the action, withdrawing from it in order to observe it from above and from a distance, he [the social scientist] constitutes practical activity as an *object of observation and analysis*, a *representation*.[6]

It is the initial act of assuming a position of detachment from the world under study which lies at the heart of the objectivist—subjectivist dualism which Bourdieu finds so unacceptable. More correctly, perhaps, it is the objective–subjective distinction, the epistemological and emotional well-spring of the western scientific endeavour – the Enlightenment project of rationalism – which creates the possibility of taking up a detached view of the social world in the first place. Thus is created the notion of 'two ways of looking at things' – one more scientific, more authoritative than the other – which offers the false choice, according to Bourdieu, of *either* one way *or* the other. Given the privileged epistemological authority accorded to objectivity there is, effectively, no choice: hence, at the end of the day, the detached stance of the observer.

When Bourdieu says that the observer 'tends to bring into the object the principles of his relations to the object', what he means is this: as an outside observer, the anthropologist tries to make sense of the action, looking for rules with which to understand what is going on. This quest proceeds largely on the basis of verbal communication with the actors. The kind of questions which an observer will ask are likely to produce normative, value-oriented statements about what it is believed *ought* to happen, rather than a valid description of 'what goes on'.

In addition, however, Bourdieu seems to be saying something else.[7] Two things, to be precise. First, he argues that the second step backwards, epistemologically speaking, is necessary in order to reveal or unmask the techniques of the observer: codification, visualisation in charts and diagrams, etc. All of these devices serve to set in explanatory concrete something – social life – which is, *in its very nature*, fluid, diachronic and mobile. Sociology and anthropology thus become more like the forensic science of the autopsy than anything else.

In the second place, Bourdieu suggests a means whereby these problems can be overcome, for avoiding the false choice between the unreal intimacy of a subjectivist position – an essentially descriptive model of the social world as it is believed to be experienced – or the equally misleading superiority of objectivism, the search for the sociological equivalent of Descartes' mechanical universe, functioning according to rules, if not laws.

He does not dismiss either option completely; in fact, Bourdieu's is an attempt to preserve the gains made by each.[8] If nothing else, each can offer a necessary and constructive critique of the other. They also each have their positive virtues. On the one hand, there is the desire for explanatory pattern and order and the recognition that people have only an imperfect knowledge and understanding of the world and their place in it. Hence the need for a view from 'above'. On the other hand, there is the importance and value of what people know as a resource for social science and the undefined human capacity for making life up, from moment to moment. Hence, the need for a view from 'below'. In terms of Bourdieu's intellectual history there is, on one side, structuralism (objectivism) and, on the other, existentialism (subjectivism).

Here we come back to Bourdieu's alternative to this 'ruinous' epistemological opposition, an approach which he has described as 'participant objectivation'. This involves a double distancing – the 'two steps back' which we have already discussed. First, there is the work done in the act of observation and the objectification or distortion of social reality which it is likely to produce. Second, there is an awareness of that distortion and of the observer as a competent social actor in his/her own right. As competent, in appropriate context, as the actors who are being studied. It is this awareness which allows the objectivity of the observer to be creatively maintained while, at the same time, permitting an imaginative leap into the shoes of the objects of study (i.e. research *subjects* – the terminological confusion here is, I suspect, more than coincidental). Bourdieu asks us to recognise that just as *we* are neither rule-governed automata, precisely and unconsciously orchestrated by our culture, nor, at the other extreme, comprehensively knowledgeable, neither are *they*:

> I have no polemical axe to grind in pointing out that the anthropologist would probably give a better account of rituals of kinship relations if he introduced into his theory the 'understanding' – in Wittgenstein's sense of the ability to use them correctly – that is evident in his relations with the founding fathers of the discipline or his skill at performing the social rituals of academic life.[9]

> The distinction between sociology and ethnology prevents the ethnologist from submitting his own experience to the analysis that he applies to his object. This would oblige him to discover that what he describes as mythical thought is, quite frequently, nothing other than the practical logic we apply in three out of four of our own actions . . .[10]

This is Bourdieu's version of the notion of the psychic unity of mankind. Cultures may divide the peoples of the earth, but in their relation to culture – how they learn it, handle it, modify it, draw upon it as a resource – they have more in common than not. Hence Bourdieu's interest in how things are done, in *practice*: it is not possible to read other minds, but it may be possible to step into other shoes.

Which is where we return to experiments in epistemology, rendering the mundane exotic and vice versa. Bourdieu's con-

frontation with his own social world(s) led him to two reali-
sations: that the act of observation, pursued unreflexively, produces a static, reified and unreal view of social life, and that
social practice – and here his privileged status as insider *as well*
as outsider produced its dividend – is composed of strategic
vagueness and tactical improvisation, rather than the adherence
to rules or recipes. The first intuition distinguishes his subsequent
work from the objectivism of structuralism or positivistic empiricism.[11] The second serves to differentiate his sociology from
the subjectivist heirs of existentialism, phenomenology and ethnomethodology in particular.[12]

Both of these objectionable alternatives are, however, similar
in important respects. Both options – objectivism and subjectivism – are theoretical modes of knowledge, each in their own way
at a considerable distance from the practical knowledge of actors
and each, because of their inability to make the second step
back – the epistemological break with routine scientific modes
of apprehension which is the key to Bourdieu's argument and
originality[13] – incapable of understanding that practical knowledge. So far as Bourdieu is concerned, they cannot understand
the social world at all.

It is this attempt to thread a dialectical middle way or third
path between the thesis and antithesis of objectivism and subjectivism which distinguishes Bourdieu's project. By objectifying the
position of the social scientist as a competent actor in his/her own
social world(s), as well as the position of the research subjects, it
is possible to place both observer and observed within the same
epistemological frame. By doing research on his own doorstep
he could not avoid doing this, and thus was the epistemological
break made.

There are three brief points to be made here by way of commentary on this chapter so far. The first has to do with the words
objective and *subjective*. In standard usage they bear a number
of meanings: Bourdieu takes advantage of this polysemy, but he
does so without clarification. Given his approach to language,
which will be the focus of Chapter Seven's discussion, this is
perhaps only to be expected. For our purposes, however, a little
light should perhaps be shed on the situation. In the first place,
he talks about objectivism and subjectivism: these as we have
seen are epistemological alternatives, different ways of knowing
the social world. Then, however, as in 'the subjective expectation
of objective probability', he is referring to different classes or

kinds of social phenomena. There is the invisible world of what goes on in people's heads, what they think, and then there is the social world outside them, the world in which history, social structure and unifying pattern are to be found. This latter is, for Bourdieu, the 'real' world; 'objective' is, therefore, a gloss for 'true'. These are distinctions which lie in the nature of things; in the language of philosophy they are to do with ontology rather than epistemology. Finally, he talks about objectification, the process of constituting the social world as an object of analytical attention through a process of detachment and distancing. These different meanings should be kept clearly in view when reading Bourdieu. As we shall see in the next chapter, they serve to mask important contradictions in his thinking.

Second, the notion of the 'objectification of objectification' seems to include two rather different – although not contradictory – things. Easiest to understand, and less radical, is the notion that sociologists should be reflexive about the categories they employ, their research methods and the procedures which they adopt in order to constitute social life as available for analysis. Only thus can they hope to distinguish between what is actually 'in the data' and what may be an artifact of the research process. More difficult is the notion of 'participant objectivation', an equally important element of Bourdieu's 'epistemological experimentation'. As already discussed, this involves a substantial epistemological break with the characteristic detachment of research. It is not always clear which of these options Bourdieu has in mind when he talks about objectifying objectification.

The third point has to do with the distinction between sociology and anthropology (or, in much French usage, ethnology). Bourdieu is probably wrong to suggest that it is easier for the sociologist than the anthropologist to analyse his or her own experience in the same way that they analyse the experience of others. Most sociologists are markedly distanced, in terms of either class, ethnicity or gender, from their research subjects. The situation is less extreme than that encountered by most anthropologists but the difference is of degree, not kind. In fact, the illusion of a limited commensality between researcher and subject – a common enough illusion in sociology – may actually be a further barrier in the way of the epistemological break which Bourdieu is proposing.[14]

OFFICIAL ACCOUNTS

I have already mentioned Bourdieu's argument that a research strategy which consists largely of eliciting from informants accounts of and for their behaviour will produce a misleading picture of social life. The 'of and for' is important: the native accounts in question tend to describe the state of affairs which *ought* to happen because the nature of the occasion inspires them to explain (or justify) their behaviour, in addition to (or instead of) describing it. The accounts which they produce are thus 'official accounts'.

As research data, Bourdieu argues that there are three things wrong with what research subjects may say in their answers to a social scientist's questions.[15] First, as a 'discourse of familiarity' it takes much for granted, and much that is important. It is all that goes without saying, the tacit assumptions which are the *sine qua non* of everyday life, which is left unsaid. Second, as an 'outsider-oriented discourse' it will tend to remain couched at the level of the general, eschewing the detail of particular cases and situations. This is because the informant will presume the questioner's unfamiliarity with the social world in question, something which is, of course, clear from the uninformed nature of the questions being asked. Third, the discourse of informants reflects a 'semi-theoretical disposition', itself the product of 'learned questioning'. Rationalisations, located within a framework of 'juridical, ethical, or grammatical formalism', are the product of the informant's desire to impress, to demonstrate a mastery of the topic in question. This also motivates the informant to dwell on the best and the worst – the 'most esteemed or reprehended' – extremes of the spectrum of possibilities. Worst of all, however, is the constant recourse in such accounts to a vocabulary of rules – 'the language of grammar, morality and law' – to describe social practice that is, according to Bourdieu, the outcome of a tacit, unreflexive, practical knowledge.

Bourdieu's point, therefore, is about the nature of the research process *and* about the inability of actors adequately to reflect upon their own practice. Practical mastery, interactional accomplishment or competence in any given situation, depends upon a great deal being taken for granted and implicit;[16] it is, therefore, literally too much to ask to expect informants to lay bare the principles which structure that ongoing social situation.

In addition, however, Bourdieu is also saying something about the questioner:

> Native theories are dangerous not so much because they lead research towards illusory explanations as because they bring quite superfluous reinforcement to the intellectualist tendency inherent in the objectivist approach to practices.[17]

Here we have 'the objectification of objectification' at work. Bourdieu the ethnographer is reflecting upon the testimony of informants, not only as a product of their own existences but also as an artifact of the research relationship and objectivism. Further, he also points out the mutually confirming interaction between the folk models of natives and the analytical or theoretical predilections of the social scientist.

Although Bourdieu's epistemological reflections are located largely in his anthropological works (specifically *Outline of a Theory of Practice* and *The Logic of Practice*), it is clear from other passages that they are of equal relevance to his work as a sociologist. This is particularly apparent in the context of his discussions of the French system of higher education.[18] It is equally clear that his epistemological critique is at its sharpest with respect to research which is heavily or completely dependent on in-depth interviewing, whether formal or informal, structured or unstructured. This is the research approach which is most likely to generate the 'official' native accounts of which Bourdieu is so distrustful.

So what of other research styles, in particular either participant observation or purely statistical research? Since the place and use of statistics in Bourdieu's work is discussed elsewhere in this chapter, I shall confine my attention here to participant observation. This is, he says, 'in a sense, a contradiction in terms (as anyone who has tried to do it will have confirmed in practice)'.[19] All the erstwhile participant observer manages to achieve is the worst of two possible worlds:

> One cannot *live* the belief associated with profoundly different conditions of existence, that is, with other games and other stakes, still less give others the means of reliving it by the sheer power of discourse . . . Those who want to believe with the beliefs of others grasp

neither the objective truth nor the subjective experience of belief.[20]

Much hinges on how one defines participant observation, and Bourdieu here is adopting – albeit implicitly – a particularly strong definition. His model of participant observation is one in which a genuine degree of participant comprehension[21] can, ideally, be attained: in which the ethnographer can 'get inside the skin' of his or her research subjects, thinking as they think.

This model is both a legitimate target for Bourdieu's criticism and something of a straw man. His critique is legitimate to the extent that the epistemological authority of anthropology, in particular, derives from the anthropologist's claim to be a 'marginal native'.[22] Fieldwork entails an epistemological stance as well as being a professional rite of passage. In the final analysis the claim to valid anthropological knowledge may be translated as, 'I know, because I was there', as is clear from the tenor and rhetorical egocentricity of the kind of discussion which often follows anthropological seminar papers.[23] This epistemology also helps to explain the regrettable degree to which anthropologists are prone to over-identify with, and become proprietorial about, 'their' people.

This strong model of participant observation is also, however, a straw man, and for several reasons. First, because most of the time – certainly in their written ethnographies – anthropologists work with a weaker model of participation. The stress is placed on their creative marginality and the capacity to combine something of an insider's view – and there are many different perspectives on the degree to which this is possible and how it may be achieved – with the objectivity of an outsider's perspective. The second reason is implicit in the first: there is a continuum of meanings and research styles attached to the notion of participant observation.[24] Bourdieu is arbitrarily – and somewhat literally – recognising only one possibility. In the third place, most ethnographers, be they sociologists or anthropologists, tend to be wider ranging in their use of data-generating strategies. A cheerful promiscuity of method – from the social survey to observation to unstructured interviewing to the use of videotape – is more the rule than the exception. However one defines participant observation, it generally takes its place alongside other strategies or techniques.

Finally, Bourdieu's critique leaves open the question of

participant observation in one's own culture, and here we return to his epistemological experiment. How narrow does the cultural and social distance between researcher and subject have to be before such an experiment is possible? Did Bourdieu genuinely share enough with the Béarnais peasantry to disarm the comment that he could not possibly know, in the practical sense to which he attaches so much importance, what their lives really *were* (as opposed to what they were *like*)? How much does adopting the researcher's stance towards one's own social world change one's place and position within and towards that world? Did Bourdieu's engagement with critical research on the French university system transform him into something of an outsider, undermining his epistemological claim to the legitimate practical knowledge which underwrites, and derives from, membership?

In both of these cases my sympathies are with Bourdieu's project of 'participant objectivation'. Nonetheless, the above questions remain to be posed, even if they do not necessarily demand a firm answer. Further questions are also raised about the degree to which the testimony of research subjects is, by definition, unreliable and about the limits within which they can reflect adequately upon their own practice. Bourdieu overstates the case massively here and at the risk of an epistemological conceit which – despite his protestations to the contrary[25] – privileges analytical understanding as ineluctably superior to the native understanding of the world, in a manner which is reminiscent of structuralism itself. With respect to the analysis of practice – in the highly specific way in which he defines it and is interested in it (see Chapter Four) – Bourdieu is probably correct: informants' statements *are* of limited value. However, there is a whole range of research interests and perspectives where this is not the case. It *is* possible to undertake research which must, perforce, rely largely on informants' statements about what they do, without producing little more than a sociological version of 'official accounts'.[26]

THE SYNOPTIC ILLUSION

There are all sorts of cognitive devices – metaphor and analogy are good examples – which we use to structure and produce our knowledge of the world. Synopsis is one of the most common and important: the simplification and condensation of complex information into a unified frame of reference. It is an operation which is common to both everyday discourse and the discourse of social scientists. Bourdieu's discussion of the 'synoptic illusion' derives from his dissatisfaction with structuralism and is largely concerned with three specific kinds of synoptic accounts or presentations: diagrams, genealogies and calendars.

The diagrams he has in mind are those constructed by the sociologist or anthropologist: the annual cycle of Kabyle women's activities[27] or the 'variants of petit-bourgeois taste' in France,[28] for example. Here the intention is to render visible in two-dimensional space the logical relationships between specific social phenomena: activities, expressed preferences, cultural categories, or whatever. Bourdieu suggests that there are four distinct problems with this mode of representation.

First, the relationships created between things are often an artifact of the exercise of the diagram's production; they do not exist in practice. Because these relationships never actually occur in interaction, what appears to be logically incompatible 'on paper' may be compatible in practice.[29] The entire diagrammatic creation is a kind of fiction. Second, synopsis – and this is implicit in the first point – also does violence to time. The calendrical diagram is, not surprisingly perhaps, the example *par excellence* of this:

> . . . a calendar substitutes a linear, homogeneous, continuous time for practical time, which is made up of incommensurable islands of duration, each with its own rhythm, the time that flies by or drags, depending on what one is *doing*, i.e. on the functions conferred on it by the activity in progress.[30]

Here we have the social scientific disenchantment of the world (and, indeed, what else could social science possibly be?). In the synoptic process all sense of the playing out of strategies in practice is lost, although there is apparently, in some diagrams – as, for example in Bourdieu's most recent discussion of Kabyle honour-related transactions[31] – the possibility of constructing a simple generative model which preserves the fluidity of practical logic.

Third, it is important to note the centrality of synopsis to the official accounts discussed in the previous section. This is perhaps most obviously the case with genealogies – after all, it is not only anthropologists who have an interest in kinship relations: *official* accounts of kinship, couched in a vocabulary of rules, are important rhetorical resources in the ongoing progress of *practical* kinship strategies.[32] A marriage 'rule', for example, may be used as a legitimation of some unions; its setting aside, in other circumstances, may be a potent move in a game of competitive advantage and disadvantage. Furthermore, in general, the act of questioning about kinship relations encourages the production of just such official rhetoric, which then becomes the basis of the anthropologist's genealogical chart. Finally, and it is perhaps a trivial point, the construction of synoptic presentations of data creates the risk of lapsing into the errors of structuralism – whether in the eye of the writer or the reader.[33]

The synoptic illusion also has its positive side, although it only becomes apparent when the process is viewed as an artifice, from the distance of objectification, the double distancing mentioned earlier.[34] Mundanely, there are presentational advantages – a lot of information can be presented in short compass – provided the effects of synopsis as a theoretical construction of social reality, rather than a simple description, are kept firmly in view. More significantly, it exposes the analytical difficulties in reducing practice to linear series or diagrammatic totality:

> The 'grouping of factual material' performed by the diagram . . . removes the advantage one has when manipulating separate relationships, as and when they occur to intuition, by forcing one to relate each opposition to all the others.
>
> It is this very property of the synoptic diagram that led me to discover the limits of the logic imminent in the practices which it sought to make manifest. . .the logic of practices can only be grasped through constructs which destroy it as such . . .[35]

The synoptic illusion of coherent, structured, logically organised cultural form actually reveals the fact that actors cannot possibly understand or handle its symphonic logic, that their practical logic is limited, situational and, at best, semi-conscious. Successful practice, in fact, as a tacit and intuitive accomplishment, specifically excludes a mastery of its own logic. Here we have, once again, the 'objectification of objectification': Bourdieu turns the distortions and shortcomings of synopsis to his own advantage, turning a presentational sow's ear into an analytical silk purse.

This is as good an example as one could wish for of the

complex inter-relationship in Bourdieu's work of epistemology, practical method and theorising. The theoretical insight into the nature of practice, of which more in Chapter Four, is bound up with the epistemological critique of method: this is the pay-off of Bourdieu's insistence upon the grounding of theory in empirical research.

Finally, as Bourdieu himself has recognised,[36] simply representing social reality in written form – in other words, all sociology and anthropology texts of the slightest empirical bent – is itself a synoptic procedure. What, then, are the possibilities of avoiding illusion in our analyses of social life? Can the process become sufficiently self-conscious and reflexive, sufficiently objectified, or is distortion an inescapable fact of life if one is writing social science? This is something to which I will return in Chapter Seven; Bourdieu offers a solution to the quandary, albeit one which poses further problems with respect to the politics of communication.

THE USE OF STATISTICS

It is hard to tell whether Bourdieu's emphasis upon practice – what people *do* – is cause or effect of his readiness to use statistics. He has used statistics, indeed even relied upon them, since his very earliest published studies of Algeria. By his own account, it is clear that it was statistical information about marriage patterns in Algeria which subsequently triggered off his critique of rule-governed models of social life and, eventually, of structuralism itself.[37]

The gathering and interpretation of statistics is one way of knowing the social world; the collection and analysis of accounts is another. Bourdieu is not rejecting the latter. He is arguing for a reflexive epistemological pluralism which self-consciously juxtaposes different modes or kinds of sociological (or anthropological) knowledge, although, he does privilege one kind of knowledge – the objectivity of statistics, which, as it were, represents what *really* happens – over another, the subjectivity of accounts. However, he does not forget that *both* kinds of knowledge are, nevertheless and always, representations:

> To consider regularity, that is, what recurs with a certain statistically measurable *frequency*, as the product of a consciously laid-down and consciously respected *ruling*

> . . . or as the product of an unconscious *regulating* by a
> mysterious cerebral and/or social mechanism, is to slip
> from the model of reality to the reality of the model.[38]

Bourdieu is interested in a model of reality, and statistics are
the primary datum for determining what that reality – social
practice – is. This epistemological choice is inextricably bound
up with the relationship between theory and method in Bourdieu's work; it remains difficult, and ultimately irrelevant, to
unravel the priority which each of these things has, as the quotation immediately above suggests.

One essential point about Bourdieu's use of statistics, in the
technical sense, is that it is basically descriptive; his objective
is not the complex speculation about cause and effect which
characterises techniques such as regression or log linear analysis.
It is simpler than that. Even in his statistically elaborate research
on cultural tastes or French academia the basic method usually
involves no more than the sophisticated calculation of strength
of association between various data.[39] For Bourdieu the collection and analysis of statistical data is simply the starting point,
the sociological constitution of the thing to be explained.

There are a number of criticisms to which his use of statistics
is vulnerable. It does appear, at times, to be a little cavalier,
with data from questions which are 'less classifying' (does this
mean inconvenient for the analysis?) simply being discarded.[40]
Since Bourdieu is probably admitting here to no more than the
commonplace pragmatism of all research this is, however, a
minor point. Less minor are two further criticisms. First, as in
the case of the example of Arab marriage statistics, he may be
overconfident that his statistics actually represent what they purport to represent. Statistics, as all students of research methods
are taught (or *should* be taught), are theoretically and socially
constructed phenomena, and must be interpreted as such. They
are also extreme examples of synopsis at work, with all sorts of
distortions and deceptions hidden within them. Second, much of
the survey data which Bourdieu draws upon in his sociological
studies of France are actually synoptic presentations of respon-
dents' *accounts* of their preferences, habits, etc. His confident
reliance upon them as a 'model of reality' may, therefore, be
misplaced.

In this, Bourdieu is revealing a residual positivism which is
related to his emphasis upon practice and which may be unavoid-

able. It is also an aspect of his inclination to favour the 'objective' pole of the objective–subjective opposition, an inclination which has been gradually revealed as this chapter has progressed. Underlying his sociology is a firm faith in the existence of a bedrock of social reality – the visible world of what people do – which is objectively 'real'. Despite his stated aim of doing so, he has yet, perhaps, to actually transcend the 'rock-bottom antinomy' of objectivism and subjectivism.[41]

To reiterate a by now familiar point, it is the close linkage which exists in Bourdieu's writings between theory and empirical research – and the two come together most intimately in his epistemological reflections – which is one of his greatest strengths. His epistemological critique informs and is informed by his theoretical emphasis upon practice, on the one hand, and his choices of method and experience of research, on the other.

Central to the issues raised has been his insistence upon reflexivity – 'the objectification of objectification' – as a necessary aspect of the research process. Only, if you like, by subjecting the practice of the researcher to the same critical and sceptical eye as the practice of the researched is it possible to aspire to conduct properly objective and 'scientific' research. Only by doing this is it possible to hope to understand social reality properly.

In arguing this case, Bourdieu is being neither radical nor original. The last twenty years have witnessed an increasingly sophisticated debate within sociology and anthropology about how it is possible to understand the social world and the role and importance of reflexivity in doing so.[42] Where his significance lies in this respect is in the degree to which he lays open for inspection in his work – leaving aside until later the problem of the nature of the language in which he does so – the process of reflection involved and the interplay between theory, method and epistemology. There are few other sociologists or anthropologists whose work even comes close (Clifford Geertz, for example, might be one of his competitors, and perhaps Aaron Cicourel). It is not, however, that Bourdieu's answers to the problems which he tackles are 'right' – whatever, in this context, that might mean. It is the nature of the problems which he raises, and the manner in which his work encourages his audience to tackle them, as it were, for themselves, that makes his work so important. To repeat myself, Bourdieu is 'good to think with'.

Having sketched out the epistemological terrain over which Bourdieu's theoretical development has taken place, I shall now move on to elaborate upon his theoretical arguments. Chapter Four will be concerned with practice, habitus and social fields. In proceeding to this discussion, however, the discussion of the present chapter should always be kept in mind: for Bourdieu, theory, epistemological reflection and empirical research go hand in hand. In their integration, whether one agrees with what he has to say or not, he has few rivals.

NOTES AND REFERENCES

[1] Among various student introductions to epistemological issues as they affect sociology and anthropology, see: J. Hughes, *The Philosophy of Social Research*, second edition, London, Longman (1990). The best introduction to these issues in a wider context is probably still: R. Harre, *The Philosophies of Science*, London, Oxford University Press (1972).

[2] L.D. Wacquant, 'Towards a Reflexive Sociology: A Workshop with Pierre Bourdieu', *Sociological Theory*, vol. 7 (1989), p. 33.

[3] With respect to discussions of Bourdieu's epistemology, the following exceptions are useful: G.L. Acciaiol, 'Knowing What You Are Doing: Pierre Bourdieu's "Outline of a Theory of Practice"', *Canberra Anthropology*, vol. 4 (1981), pp. 23–51; R. Harker, C. Maher and C. Wilkes (eds), *An Introduction to the Work of Pierre Bourdieu*, London, Macmillan (1990), pp. 58–85. It appears to be the case that Bourdieu himself regards this aspect of his *oeuvre* as of preeminent significance: *The Logic of Practice*, Cambridge, Polity (1990), p. 15.

[4] P. Bourdieu, *In Other Words*, Cambridge, Polity (1990), pp. 59–60; L.D. Wacquant, 'Towards a Reflexive Sociology', *op. cit.*, pp. 32–5.

[5] P. Bourdieu, *The Logic of Practice*, *op. cit.*, p. 27.

[6] P. Bourdieu, *Outline of a Theory of Practice*, Cambridge, Cambridge University Press (1977), p. 2.

[7] P. Bourdieu, *Outline of a Theory of Practice*, *op. cit.*, pp. 1–30; *In Other Words*, *op. cit.*, pp. 59–86; *The Logic of Practice*, *op. cit.*, pp. 1–42.

[8] P. Bourdieu, *The Logic of Practice*, *op. cit.*, p. 25.

[9] *Ibid.*, p. 18.

[10] P. Bourdieu, *In Other Words*, *op. cit.*, p. 66.

[11] See, for example, Bourdieu's comments on the quantitative tradition in American social science exemplified by Lazarsfeld: *In Other Words*, *op. cit.*, pp. 19–21.

[12] On ethnomethodology, see: P. Bourdieu, *Outline of a Theory . . .*, *op. cit.*, pp. 21–2, 78–81.

[13] R.Harker *et al.* (eds), *An Introduction to the Work of Pierre Bourdieu*, *op. cit.*, p. 72.

[14] The relationship between personal experience and research experience has been most interestingly raised in recent years by feminist scholars: W. Hollway, *Subjectivity and Method in Psychology: Gender, Meaning and Science*, London, Sage (1989); D.E. Smith, *The Everyday World as Problematic: A Feminist Sociology*, Milton Keynes, Open University Press (1987). Within British social anthropology, some of these issues emerge in A. Jackson (ed.), *Anthropology at Home*, London, Tavistock (1987), particularly the chapter by M. Strathern.

[15] P. Bourdieu, *Outline of a Theory . . .*, *op. cit.*, pp. 18–19.

[16] P. Bourdieu, *Outline of a Theory . . .*, *op. cit.*, pp. 16–22; *The Logic of Practice*, *op. cit.*, pp. 81–97.

[17] P. Bourdieu, *Outline of a Theory . . .*, *op. cit.*, p. 19.

[18] P. Bourdieu, *Homo Academicus*, Cambridge, Polity (1988), pp. 6–35; L.D. Wacquant, 'Towards a reflexive sociology', *op.cit.*, pp. 32–7.

[19] P. Bourdieu, *The Logic of Practice*, *op. cit.*, p. 34.

[20] *Ibid.*, p. 68.

[21] See: H.M. Collins, 'Researching Spoonbending: Concepts and Practice of Participatory Fieldwork', in C. Bell and H. Roberts (eds), *Social Researching*, London, Routledge and Kegan Paul (1984).

[22] On the epistemological claims of anthropologists to be 'marginal natives', see, for example: C. Geertz, ' "From the Nature's Point of View": On the Nature of Anthropological Understanding', in K.M. Basso and H.A. Selby (eds), *Meaning in Anthropology*, Albuquerque, University of New Mexico Press (1976); L. Holy and M. Stuchlik, *Actions, Norms and Representations*, Cambridge, Cambridge University Press (1983), pp. 74–80.

[23] I am referring here to the 'bongo-bongoism' of much informal anthropological argument – of the kind, for example,

that occurs after departmental seminars – in which the point being made is frequently preceded by a statement something like, 'Among the. . .'.

[24] On the range of different meanings of participant observation, see H.M. Collins, 'Researching Spoonbending', *op.cit.*

[25] P. Bourdieu, *In Other Words*, *op. cit.*, p. 9, is an example.

[26] See: L. Holy and M. Stuchlik, *Actions, Norms and Representations*, *op. cit.* For a discussion of the possibility of conducting research when informants' accounts of their practice are the major information source, see: R. Jenkins, 'Doing Research into Discrimination', in G.C. Wenger (ed.), *The Research Relationship*, London, Allen and Unwin (1987). For a critique of this argument, see: D.L. Collinson, D. Knights and M. Collinson, *Managing to Discriminate*, London, Routledge (1990), pp. 62–3, 227–8.

[27] P. Bourdieu, *The Logic of Practice*, *op. cit.*, p. 248.

[28] P. Bourdieu, *Distinction*, London, Routledge and Kegan Paul (1984), p. 340.

[29] Bourdieu, *Outline of a Theory* . . ., *op. cit.*, p. 107.

[30] *Ibid.*, p. 105.

[31] P. Bourdieu, *The Logic of Practice*, *op. cit.*, pp. 100–101.

[32] P. Bourdieu, *Outline of a Theory* . . ., *op. cit.*, pp. 33–71; *The Logic of Practice*, *op. cit.*, pp. 147–99.

[33] P. Bourdieu, *Outline of a Theory* . . ., *op. cit.*, p. 219, n.6.

[34] P. Bourdieu, *The Logic of Practice*, *op. cit.*, p. 201.

[35] *Ibid.*, pp. 10, 11.

[36] P. Bourdieu, *In Other Words*, *op. cit.*, pp. 100–101; *The Logic of Practice*, *op. cit.*, p. 11.

[37] P. Bourdieu, *In Other Words*, *op. cit.*, p. 8; A. Honneth, H. Kocyba and B. Schwibs, 'The Struggle for Symbolic Order: An Interview with Pierre Bourdieu', *Theory, Culture and Society*, vol. 3 no. 3 (1986), p. 40.

[38] P. Bourdieu, *Outline of a Theory* . . ., *op. cit.*, p. 29.

[39] P. Bourdieu, *Distinction*, *op. cit.*, pp. 503–18; *Homo Academicus*, *op. cit.*, pp. 69–72. The exception is his work, with A. Darbel and D. Schnapper, on the public use of art galleries, in which complicated mathematical models, deriving from economics, are constructed to predict the probability that different categories of the population, identified as possessing different amounts of formal cultural capital, will use galleries: *The Love of Art*, Cambridge, Polity

(1991), pp. 73–85. As with much economics, this, the work of Darbel, exhibits a superficial sophistication which conceals an underlying theoretical naivety.

[40] P. Bourdieu, *Distinction*, *op. cit.*, p. 261.

[41] P. Bourdieu, '*Vive la crise*! For Heterodoxy in Social Science', *Theory and Society*, vol. 17 (1988), p. 780.

[42] There is now a huge literature reflecting, in one way or another and with vastly different degrees of sophistication, upon the research process and the sociological enterprise. In addition to the literature cited in notes [14] and [22], above, see: A. Bryman, *Quantity and Quality in Social Research*, London, Unwin Hyman (1988); C. Fletcher, *Beneath the Surface*, London, Routledge and Kegan Paul (1974); M. Herzfeld, *Anthropology Through the Looking-Glass*, Cambridge, Cambridge University Press (1987). The last work cited draws, it must be admitted, a considerable amount of its inspiration from Bourdieu. More generally, the reader is recommended to look at the seminal contributions of Alvin Gouldner; for example, *The Coming Crisis of Western Sociology*, London, Heinemann (1971), pp. 20–60, 481–512.

4

Practice, Habitus and Field

The central plank in Bourdieu's sociological platform is his attempt to transcend the 'compulsory' and 'ritual' choice between subjectivism and objectivism. In rejecting the determinism of mechanistic explanations of social life, however, he does not want to fall into the other trap, as he perceives it, of viewing conscious and deliberate intentions as a sufficient explanation of what people do. To adopt Hollis's terminology this is the distinction between plastic man and autonomous man: 'Where Plastic Man has his causes, Autonomous Man has his reasons'.[1] It can be assimilated to a series of homologous oppositions, 'the individual versus society, action versus structure, freedom versus necessity, etc.',[2] which provide the contemporary theoretical debate about structuration with its problematic and *raison d'être*.[3] It is in terms of this theoretical ambition that Bourdieu's contribution to sociology and anthropology must be assessed. This is the criterion against which he offers himself for judgement.

In assessing that contribution, however, a further important point to bear in mind is Bourdieu's rejection of the project of 'grand theory'. Theory for its own sake, for example, is roundly dismissed:

> Let me say outright and very forcefully that I never 'theorise', if by that we mean engage in the kind of conceptual gobbledygook . . . that is good for textbooks and which, through an extraordinary misconstrual of the logic of science, passes for Theory in much of Anglo-American social science . . . There is no doubt a theory in my work, or, better, a set of *thinking tools* visible through the results they yield, but it is not built as such . . . It is a *temporary construct which takes shape for and by empirical work*.[4]

In this chapter, three of Bourdieu's most important 'thinking tools' – the concepts of practice, habitus and field – will be discussed. However, regardless for the moment of whether or not Bourdieu writes the kind of conceptual gobbledygook that passes for theory in much of *French* social science, in refusing to identify himself as a theoretician, Bourdieu is being too modest. For one thing, he regularly uses the word 'theory' in describing his own work: *Outline of a Theory of Practice*, for example, or 'Elements for a Theory of the Political Field', the sub-title of Chapter Eight of *Language and Symbolic Power*. Bourdieu is too sophisticated to throw around carelessly a world like 'theory'. More substantially, however – and it is one of the themes of this book – Bourdieu's intellectual project is longstanding, relatively coherent and cumulative. It amounts to nothing less than an attempt to construct a theory of social practice and society. It is emphatically *not* a 'temporary construct' subordinate to the needs of empirical research. On the basis of his own and others' empirical work, the one informed by and informing the other, Bourdieu has developed a body of social theory which is worthy of detailed discussion in its own right. It is to this discussion that we will now turn.

PRACTICE AND ITS LOGIC

Bourdieu's focus upon the visible social world of practice is not particularly novel. Under a variety of subtly different rubrics – social interaction, everyday life, social behaviour, or whatever – it has always been a staple of the empirical diet of sociology and social anthropology. Where the importance of Bourdieu's project lies is in his attempt to construct a *theoretical* model of social practice, to do more than simply take what people do in their daily lives for granted, and to do so without losing sight of the wider patterns of social life. The difficulties which he encounters in doing so are a lesson to us all.

His approach to theorising social practice is distinguished in the first instance by a series of emphases: upon the establishment of a statistical pattern of 'reality' as a basic datum; upon problematising what people say as something other than either simply a reflection of 'what is going on in their heads' or a valid description of the social world; upon the improvisatory and strategic nature of practice, as opposed to viewing behaviour as governed by rules; and upon the necessity for a diachronic analysis which situates the ebb and flow of social life in time and space.

As the discussion in Chapter Three illustrates, these features of Bourdieu's model of practice must be understood within the context of his epistemological critique of social research. In particular, the key notions of 'participant objectivation' and 'the objectification of objectification' are essential if the reader is to properly understand what Bourdieu is talking about. He is trying to understand his own practice as much as anyone else's.

It is possible, however, to identify influences upon Bourdieu's thinking about practice other than epistemological experimentation. In particular, he has admitted a debt to Marx, specifically the Marx of the *Theses on Feuerbach*.[5] Indeed, one only has to look at the *Theses* to see how this might be so: 'All social life is essentially *practical*. All the mysteries which lead theory towards mysticism find their rational solution in human practice and in the comprehension of this practice.'[6] It could almost be Bourdieu himself speaking. Of course, there are many other sources in Marx's work for ideas such as these, particularly in the *Economic and Philosophic Manuscripts of 1844* and the *Grundrisse*, and Bourdieu is well aware of them. However, his view of the role of the *Theses* in the development of his theory of practice tells us something about the man. They did not, in themselves, apparently, *inspire* him in his thinking; rather, they *encouraged* him to express his thoughts.[7] This insight reaffirms the significance of the experience of doing research, and of his epistemological reflections upon that experience, in Bourdieu's sociological development. It is also a good example of a sub-text which informs all of Bourdieu's work, namely the claim that his ideas are not only original but novel, superseding their antecedents without owing much to them.

As good a place as any to start thinking about Bourdieu's development of a theorised model of social practice is with the notion of theory itself. Every society, every culture, every group of people who recognise themselves as a collectivity, has theories about the world and their place in it: models of how the world is, of how the world ought to be, of human nature, of cosmology. These are what tend to be revealed in the 'official accounts' which form the core of informants' testimony to interested researchers. But the point to bear in mind about these accounts is that they are learned and constructed in, through and as a part of the business of everyday life. They do not simply – or even at all – fulfil purely theoretical or cognitive functions: they are about *doing* as much as they are about *knowing*. To be truer perhaps to Bourdieu's meaning, only insofar as one does things is it possible to know about things.[8]

What is therefore interesting is the disjuncture between these accounts and what people actually do. In other words, what is it that produces behaviour, if it is so clearly *not* the cultural knowledge which is revealed in 'official' public discourse? This is a question to which I will return. Before that, however, it is important to expand upon the distinctive features of practice in Bourdieu's scheme of things.

First of all, practice is located in space and, more significantly, in time. It is something that can be observed in three dimensions and, necessarily, from moment to moment. Temporality, the inexorable passage of time, is an axiomatic feature of practice: time is both a constraint and a resource for social interaction. More than that, practice is 'intrinsically defined by its *tempo*'.[9] Time, and the sense of it, is, of course, socially constructed; it is, however, socially constructed out of natural cycles – days and nights, seasons, the human pattern of reproduction, growth and ageing. Similarly, and more immediately, interaction *takes* time – and it occurs in space. Time and space are both capable of being modelled in different ways, and are thus equally social constructs, but movement in space always involves movement in time. Practice as a visible, 'objective', social phenomenon cannot be understood outside of time/space. Any adequate analysis of practice must, therefore, treat temporality as a central feature of its very nature.

Second, practice, according to Bourdieu, is not consciously –

or not *wholly* consciously – organised and orchestrated. Nothing is random or purely accidental but, as one thing follows on from another, practice happens (although, as we shall see, it would be incorrect to suggest that Bourdieu thinks that it *just* happens). What Bourdieu is attempting to get at here may best be summed up in his notions of *practical sense* or *practical logic*. Bourdieu has written about these from different directions and in different ways, but one of his most potent metaphors is the centrality of 'a feel for the game':

> the practical mastery of the logic or of the imminent necessity of a game – a mastery acquired by experience of the game, and one which works outside conscious control and discourse (in the way that, for instance, techniques of the body do).[10]

The reader may be forgiven for being reminded here of Goffman's metaphors of social life as a kind of theatre or as a game.[11] There are two sides to this practical sense, the first of which is the 'necessity imminent in the social world'.[12] This can be interpreted – in part – as a restatement of Marx's adage that, although men make their own history, they do not do so in circumstances of their own choosing. It is also, however, a comment upon the fact that actors do not just *confront* their current circumstances. They are an integral part of those circumstances. Within them they have grown up, learning and acquiring a set of practical cultural competences, including a social identity – 'the sense of the position one occupies in social space'[13] – which renders them largely incapable of perceiving social reality, in all of its arbitrariness, as anything other than 'the way things are', necessary to their own existence as *who* they are. Most people, most of the time, take themselves and their social world somewhat for granted: they do not think about it because they do not have to. Elsewhere, Bourdieu refers to this as *doxa* or 'doxic experience':

> the coincidence of the objective structures and the internalized structures which provides the illusion of immediate understanding, characteristic of practical experience of the familiar universe, and which at the same time excludes from that experience any inquiry as to its own conditions of possibility.[14]

At this point we seem to be coming back to the idea of the

'subjective expectation of objective probability'. Bourdieu's point here is more than that, however: the business of social life would not be possible unless it were taken for granted most of the time. We don't spend our time questioning the meaning of life because we cannot afford to and social imperatives do not allow – in both senses of the word – us to do it.

The other aspect of practical logic or sense is its characteristic fluidity and indeterminacy: 'the "art" of the *necessary improvisation* which defines excellence'.[15] Social life, in all of its complexity and variety, is not accomplished on the basis of rules, recipes and normative models. Imagine the impossibility, suggests Bourdieu, of having 'on file' a rule or prescription for every conceivable situation which one might encounter in routine social life.[16] The depiction of practice as an improvisatory performance brings us back to time: improvisation is the exploitation of pause, interval and indecision. Although time is objectively irreversible, delay – or, indeed its opposite, the swift execution of the surprise move – is manipulable as a strategic resource. It is not, however, that actors *choose* to improvise their way through life; no other approach could possibly work, an insight which seems to be rooted in Bourdieu's epistemological experiment, the adoption of an objective stance towards his own practice.

At this stage a substantial caveat must be entered about Bourdieu's use of the metaphor of social life as a game. First of all, one of the things that all games have is rules, and these do, to some extent, determine what players can and cannot do. The same is true of social life. Second, games are learned through explicit teaching as well as experientially in practice. So, once again, is social competence. Bourdieu, as we will see shortly, overemphasises the latter at the expense of the former. Finally, his talk about excellence ignores the fact that it is a quality which differs from mere competence and is both unevenly distributed and relatively uncommon. Most people, most of the time, exhibit, at best, competence rather than excellence in their dealings with others. Bourdieu does not help us to understand the absence of 'excellence' in social interaction, let alone the ubiquity of incompetence.

Although practice is accomplished – in Bourdieu's understanding of the social world – without conscious deliberation for the most part, it is not without its purpose(s). This is the third point and it may be summarised in Bourdieu's description of his rejection of structuralism as a theoretical move 'from rules to strategies'. The notion of strategising, to encompass the fact that actors do have goals and interests, is also designed to locate the source of their practice in their own experience of reality – their practical sense or logic – rather than in the analytical models which social scientists construct to explain that practice.[17] Whether or not Bourdieu succeeds in doing this is a question to which we will return later.

The best examples of Bourdieu's deployment of the concept of strategising are perhaps to be found in his recent discussions of the pursuit of honour in Kabylia,[18] the kinship and inheritance strategies of the Béarn peasantry[19] and Kabyle marriage patterns.[20] In these ethnographic analyses he describes the interplay of culturally 'given' dispositions, interests and ways of proceeding, on the one hand, and, on the other, individual skills and social competences, the constraints of resource limitations, the unintended consequences which intrude into any ongoing chain of transactions, personal idiosyncrasies and failings, and the weight of the history of relationships between the individuals concerned and the groups in which they claim membership.

In postulating this model of strategy and strategising, Bourdieu hopes to move away from two separate, if intimately related, dualisms. In the first place, he is attempting adequately to communicate the mixture of freedom *and* constraint which characterises social interaction. In the second, he presents practice as the product of processes which are neither wholly conscious nor wholly unconscious, rooted in an ongoing process of learning which begins in childhood, and through which actors know – without knowing – the right thing to do.[21] Taking these two points together, Bourdieu describes the practical accomplishment of successful interaction as 'second nature'.

Part of this second nature is the actors' understanding, albeit somewhere at the back of their minds, of the usual pattern of how things are done or happen: 'The regularity that can be grasped statistically, which the feel for the game spontaneously abides by, which you "recognize" practically by "playing the game". . .'.[22] Knowledge of the social world is an integral aspect of the production and reproduction of that world, even if – or especially if – it is the implicit knowledge of practical logic.

As one might expect, Bourdieu is highly critical of those social science models which depend upon a model of human behaviour as intrinsically rational and calculative. He has been particularly acerbic about Elster's work in this respect.[23] His objections to rational choice theory, or, as he prefers to describe it, RAT (rational action theory), may be summarised thus: (a) it substitutes an arbitrary rationality or interest, the pursuit of which is offered up as the well-spring of social life, for the culturally defined and historically variable rationalities and interests of real life; (b) in doing so, it substitutes the social scientist's analytical model for reality; (c) in locating the dynamic of social life in individual and conscious decision-making it ignores the individual and collective histories which unconsciously generate the ongoing reality of that social life; and (d) the methodological individualism of RAT prevents a theoretical apprehension of the relationships between individuals and between individuals and their environment which are 'the proper object of social science'.

Bourdieu goes on to argue, however, that it is easy to understand why RAT may appear to be 'empirically sound'. What is more, it is his own theoretical concept of the habitus which enables this error of appearances to be revealed:

> Individual finalism, which conceives action as determined by the conscious aiming at explicitly posed goals, is a well-founded illusion: the sense of the game which implies an anticipated adjustment of habitus to the necessities and to the probabilities inscribed in the field does present itself under the appearance of a successful 'aiming at' a future.[24]

Thus RAT is, in Bourdieu's eyes, nothing more than a sociologised version of the fond illusions which actors themselves entertain about their own rationality and powers of decision-making.[25]

One could, perhaps, interpret this as saying that although actors may understand their behaviour as the pursuit of known goals and objectives, the sociologist (Bourdieu) knows better. This in turn might be an acceptable point of view were it not for the fact that one of Bourdieu's *own* 'explicitly posed goals' is to move beyond the epistemological presumption of structuralism that the observer is privileged with respect to 'natives', who are, almost by definition, assumed to be ignorant of their own situation.[26] One is also perhaps entitled to ask Bourdieu an awkward question, apropos of epistemological experimentation and participant objectivation: if sociologists such as Bourdieu can set themselves goals and objectives, which they then pursue, why can this not also be true for their research subjects? At the very least, this question suggests that a reaction to rational decision-making models which is as hostile as Bourdieu's, risks throwing the baby out with the bath water. We know, on the basis of our own experience if nothing else, that actors do, some of the time, make decisions which they attempt to act upon and that they do, sometimes, formulate and adopt plans which they attempt to carry out. Any model or theory of social practice which does not recognise this experiential truth will be at least as flawed as the proposition that conscious decision-making is *all* we need to understand.

HABITUS

In his emphasis upon social practice, Bourdieu is concerned with what individuals do in their daily lives. He is, however, emphatic that social life cannot be understood as simply the aggregate of individual behaviour. Nor does he accept that practice can be understood solely in terms of individual decision-making, on the one hand, or as determined by supra-individual 'structures', as the metaphysics of objectivism would have it, on the other. His refinement and use of the notion of the 'habitus' is a bridge-building exercise across the explanatory gap between these two extremes, another important device for transcending the sterility of the opposition between subjectivism and objectivism.

What, then, is the habitus? What does it mean? Literally, it is a Latin word which refers to a habitual or typical condition, state or appearance, particularly of the body. In Bourdieu's appropriation of the word, it derives in the first instance from 1967 and an appendix which he contributed to his own translation into French of Panofsky's *Gothic Architecture and Scholasticism*.[27] Before that, however, it appears in a variety of settings, in, among others, the work of 'Hegel, Husserl, Weber, Durkheim and Mauss'.[28] It is 'an acquired system of generative schemes objectively adjusted to the particular conditions in which it is constituted'.[29]

Bourdieu retains some of the concept's original meaning(s) in the relationship between the body and the habitus. The dispositions and generative classificatory schemes which are the essence of the habitus are embodied in real human beings.[30] This embodiment appears to have three meanings in Bourdieu's work. First, in a trivial sense, the habitus only exists inasmuch as it is 'inside the heads' of actors (and the head is, after all, part of the body). Second, the habitus only exists in, through and because of the practices of actors and their interaction with each other and with the rest of their environment: ways of talking, ways of moving, ways of making things, or whatever. In this respect, the habitus is emphatically *not* an abstract or idealist concept. It is not just *manifest* in behaviour, it is an integral *part* of it (and vice versa). Third, the 'practical taxonomies' which were discussed in Chapter Two, and which are at the heart of the generative schemes of the habitus, are rooted in the body. Male/female, front/back, up/down, hot/cold, these are all primarily sensible – in terms of making sense and of being rooted in sensory experience – from the point of view of the embodied person.

The embodiment of the habitus finds another expression in Bourdieu's use of the word 'hexis'. Originally Greek, with a meaning not dissimilar to the Latin 'habitus', in Bourdieu's work it is used to signify deportment, the manner and style in which actors 'carry themselves': stance, gait, gesture, etc. The similarity of the original meanings of the two words, habitus and hexis, is an indication of the centrality of the body to Bourdieu's conceptualisation of the habitus. It is in bodily hexis that the idiosyncratic (the personal) combines with the systematic (the social).[31] It is the mediating link between individuals' subjective worlds and the cultural world into which they are born and which they share with others:

> Bodily hexis is political mythology realised, *em-bodied*, turned into a permanent disposition, a durable manner of standing, speaking and thereby of *feeling* and *thinking* . . . The principles em-bodied in this way are placed beyond the grasp of consciousness, and hence cannot be touched by voluntary, deliberate transformation, cannot even be made explicit . . .[32]

The example which Bourdieu uses to exemplify this point is the deportment of men and women in Kabylia: the politics of gender shape and are revealed in ways of walking, looking, even standing still. The female ideal of modesty and restraint orients her body down, towards the ground; the ideal male, however, moves upwards and outwards in his hexis, his body oriented towards other men. For Bourdieu, the body is a mnemonic device upon and in which the very basics of culture, the practical taxonomies of the habitus, are imprinted and encoded in a socialising or learning process which commences during early childhood. This differentiation between learning and socialisation is important: the habitus is inculcated as much, if not more, by *experience* as by explicit *teaching*.

The other sense in which Bourdieu's notion of the habitus retains some of the original Latin meaning is related to this last point. The power of the habitus derives from the thoughtlessness of habit and habituation, rather than consciously learned rules and principles. Socially competent performances are produced as a matter of routine, without explicit reference to a body of codified knowledge, and without the actors necessarily 'knowing what they are doing' (in the sense of being able adequately to explain what they are doing).

Looking at Bourdieu's basic definitions of the habitus, a number of things demand further consideration. What, for example, are 'dispositions'? They might be no more than 'attitudes', and indeed have often been understood as such.[33] This is, however, an inadequate understanding of the notion, although attitudes do indeed come into it. More plausible is a broader interpretation which includes a spectrum of cognitive and affective factors: thinking *and* feeling, to use Bourdieu's own formulation, everything from classificatory categories to the sense of honour.

Recognising the difficulty, perhaps, with the notion of 'disposition', Bourdieu has addressed his reasons for adopting the term in a footnote to *Outline of a Theory of Practice*.[34] The word 'disposition', he says, encompasses three distinct meanings: (a) 'the result of an organising action', a set of outcomes which he describes as approximating to 'structure'; (b) a 'way of being' or a 'habitual state'; and (c) a 'tendency', 'propensity' or 'inclination'. This exegesis makes matters more rather than less complicated – this is not an uncontradictory cluster of meanings – and probably raises more questions than it was intended to answer. For example, taking (a) at face value, dispositions appear to be identified and defined in terms of their consequences. This is, at best, tautological and, at worst, allows no scope for failed, unsuccessful or otherwise thwarted dispositions. Either way, it is much too smooth a model of social process to be convincing.

The most complicated of these questions relates to the status of dispositions with respect to the conscious and the unconscious mind. Bourdieu refers over and over again to the unconscious character of practical logic and the existence of dispositions as beyond consciousness. However, it is equally clear that consciousness *must* be involved: speech, for example, is a complicated process which involves a full range of mental/intellectual operations, both conscious and unconscious. Bourdieu himself appears to recognise this:

> Each agent, *wittingly or unwittingly*, willy nilly, is a producer and reproducer of objective meaning. . . . It is because subjects do not, strictly speaking, know what they are doing that what they do *has more meaning than they know*. [35: my emphasis]

It is difficult to know where to place conscious deliberation and awareness in Bourdieu's scheme of things. We are back with the problem of his attitude towards rational decision-making and calculation. The issue is not so much his denial of apparently calculative rationality as a social phenomenon, as his disbelief in its importance or relevance:

> The lines of action suggested by habitus may very well be accompanied by a strategic calculation of costs and benefits which tends to carry out at a conscious level the operations which habitus carries out in its own way . . . Times of crises, in which the routine adjustment of subjective and objective structures is brutally disrupted, constitute a class of circumstances when indeed 'rational choice' often appears to take over. But, and this is a crucial proviso, it is habitus itself that commands this option. We can always say that individuals make choices, as long as we do not forget that they do not choose the principals of these choices.[36]

Thus, according to Bourdieu, the surface appearance of decision-making is *either* (a) a shadow or a reflection of what the habitus is doing anyway, either beforehand or simultaneously, (b) an option which, under certain circumstances, is part of the repertoire of the habitus, not, in any sense, an autonomous or chosen process, or (c) an illusion, insofar as the principles of its operation are constrained by and derive from the habitus. At the end of the day, the less than conscious dispositions of the habitus are what produce practices.

This is what Bourdieu means when he says that the dispositions which make up the habitus are the 'generative basis' of practices. The words which Bourdieu uses suggest a causal link between the habitus and practices which is neither mechanical nor deterministic: the habitus *disposes* actors to do certain things, it provides a *basis* for the generation of practices. Practices are produced in and by the encounter between the habitus and its dispositions, on the one hand, and the constraints, demands and opportunities of the social field or market to which the habitus is appropriate or within which the actor is moving, on the other.[37] This is achieved by a less than conscious process of adjustment of the habitus and practices of individuals to the objective and external constraints of the social world.

Talk of social fields or markets brings us to the transposable quality of dispositions. By this he means the capacity of basic dispositions – particularly, I suspect, practical taxonomies – to structure and create relevance in social contexts and fields other than those in which they were originally acquired and to which they are generatively most appropriate. With respect to the habitus of the traditional Kabyle peasantry, this has been touched upon in Chapter Two: the power of gender categories to organise and imbue meaning into vast areas of social life (whether in Kabylia or elsewhere) is particularly striking. The dispositions appropriate to one field are translated according to the logic of another field.[38] This is how diverse social settings and practices exhibit a stylistic coherence or thematic unity – here we seem to be close to Weber's notion of 'elective affinity' – in the lives of embodied agents and in the life-styles of collectivities:

> . . . all the practice and products of a given agent are objectively harmonised among themselves, without any deliberate pursuit of coherence, and objectively orchestrated, without any conscious concertation, with those of all members of the same class. The habitus continuously generates practical metaphors . . . systematic transpositions required by the particular conditions in which the habitus is 'put into practice' . . . The practices of the same agent, and, more generally, the practices of all agents of the same class, owe the stylistic affinity which makes each of them a metaphor of any of the others to the fact that they are the product of transfers of the same schemes of action from one field to another.[39]

One is struck by the analogy between Bourdieu's concept of

'transposition' and the notion of 'transformation' in Lévi-Straussian structuralist analysis. There is also an affinity with Chomsky's generative model of language use, particularly his theory
of transformational grammar.[40] The contrast with Chomsky is
instructive. First, Bourdieu's dispositions are acquired through
social experience, whereas the elements and components of
Chomsky's model are presumed to be the product of human
neuro-physiology (and this, in a sense, is where Chomsky meets
Lévi-Strauss). Second, Chomsky's model offers us a mechanism,
albeit a speculative mechanism, linking deep linguistic structures
and speech practices. Bourdieu's model of the habitus is deficient
in this respect. It is not clear *how* dispositions produce practices.

Another characteristic of dispositions is that they are durable.
This is a reflection of their foundation in learning during the
early years of life, of their habitual, unreflexive nature, of their
adjustment to the objective conditions of existence, and of their
inscription in bodily hexis. These make the habitus almost
immune to major upset. Once acquired it underlies and conditions all subsequent learning and social experience.

This raises the issue of the possibility of change, both at the
individual level and the collective (because, although the habitus
is embodied in individual agents, it is a social phenomenon).
The possibility of change, in its turn, directs us to consider the
relationships between the *subjective* habitus and the *objective*
world of other people and things. Bourdieu suggests, in a characteristically elliptical and opaque formulation, that the habitus is
'the site of the internalization of reality and the externalization
of internality'.[41] Elsewhere he talks about 'the dialectical
relationship between the objective structures and the cognitive
and motivating structures which they produce and which tend to
reproduce them'.[42] Elsewhere again, we read that the habitus
is 'objectively adjusted to the particular conditions in which it
is constituted',[43] or that 'The conditionings associated with a
particular class of conditions of existence produce *habitus*'.[44]

So, we have at least three different views: objective conditions
produce the habitus, the habitus is *adjusted* to objective conditions, and there is a *reciprocal* or *dialectical* relationship
between them. Here we must distinguish between the habitus as
embodied in individuals, and the habitus as a collective, homogeneous phenomenon, mutually adjusted for and by a social
group or a class. In the first case, habitus is acquired by individuals through experience and explicit socialisation in early life.

Life and subsequent experience is then a process of adjustment between subjectivity (habitus) and objective reality.

The habitus as a shared body of dispositions, classificatory categories and generative schemes is, if it is nothing else, the outcome of collective history: 'The *habitus*, a product of history, produces individual and collective practices – more history – in accordance with the schemes generated by history.'[45] Here, once again, we have people creating their own history, albeit not in circumstances of their own choosing. The habitus cannot in any simple sense, however, be considered the cumulative 'collective wisdom' of the group (although this is doubtless true). Bourdieu is arguing that the objective world in which groups exist, and the objective environment – other people and things – as experienced from the point of view of individual members of the group, is the product of the past practices of this generation and previous generations. History culminates in an ongoing and seamless series of moments, and is continuously carried forward in a process of production and reproduction in the practices of everyday life. Here we have a process of production, a process of adjustment, and a dialectical relationship between collective history inscribed in objective conditions and the habitus inscribed in individuals. History is experienced as the taken-for-granted, axiomatic necessity of objective reality. It is the foundation of the habitus.

In this sense, history is an ongoing set of likely outcomes (probabilities). These are, however, the product of what people do (practices). In turn, practices are the product of the habitus, as well as serving to reproduce it or confirm it as 'true'. And the habitus, of course, is the ongoing culmination of history. By putting it like this, we return to the question of how the habitus produces practices. The closest which Bourdieu gets to explaining this – other than an implicit appeal to unconscious, and therefore ultimately unknowable, mental processes – is the idea of 'the subjective expectation of objective probabilities' which we discussed in Chapter Two and earlier in this chapter:

> If a very close correlation is regularly observed between the scientifically constructed objective probabilities . . . and agents' subjective aspirations . . . this is not because agents consciously adjust their aspirations to an exact evaluation of their chances of success . . . In reality, the dispositions durably inculcated by the possibilities and

impossibilities, freedoms and necessities, opportunities and prohibitions inscribed in the objective conditions . . . generate dispositions objectively compatible with these conditions and in a sense pre-adapted to their demands. The most improbable practices are therefore excluded, as unthinkable, by a kind of immediate submission to order that inclines agents to make a virtue of necessity, to refuse what is anyway denied and to will the inevitable.[46]

As a consequence, history tends to repeat itself and the *status quo* is perpetuated. This process of cultural and social reproduction is responsible for the apparent 'continuity and regularity' of social structure. Objectivist social science recognises this pattern but, according to Bourdieu, it cannot account for it, not understanding the relationship between the probabilities of the objective world and the subjective dispositions of the habitus.

This, of course, is problematic. At the least, Bourdieu is putting the cart before the horse here. In his own terms he is conflating the 'reality of the model' (probabilities) with the 'model of reality' (expectations). The former is an analytical construct, the latter rooted in the social reality under study. Bringing the two together to construct a processual mechanism which is used to explain behaviour is neither workable nor plausible. Something which happens at time 'x' cannot be accounted for by the likely state of affairs – as predicted by statistics – at time '$x + 1$'. Even if people's behaviour *is* the result of the acceptance as probable of a future which would be similar to the present, how do they learn or identify that probability? In the first instance it can only be through the internalisation (as children) of the expectations about the future articulated by significant (adult) others. It is those expectations which produce probabilities and create social reality, not the other way around.

What Bourdieu is offering here bears more than a passing resemblance to structural functionalism, and not least the structural functionalism of Talcott Parsons: social stability is the product of the internalisation of shared values, beliefs and norms. In this model of the social world, the functions of action are read off from its consequences. The comparison is a crude one and does neither Bourdieu nor Parsons any favours; provided this is recognised, however, the comparison – limited as it is – is apt.

I am not the first to identify functionalism as one of the threads in Bourdieu's theoretical tapestry. Elster, for example, has said much the same, in addition to pointing to the absence of a causal mechanism linking the habitus to what people do.[47] The two comments are related, and revolve around the place of social change in Bourdieu's thinking. As in functionalism, social change, other than as the product of external factors, is difficult to account for. Given the close, reproductive, link between the subjectivities of the habitus and the objectivity of the social world it is difficult not to perceive them as bound together in a closed feedback loop, each confirming the other. Bourdieu himself emphasises the durability of the dispositions of the habitus.

Furthermore, even if one were to accept it, it is not easy to see how this model works. The subjective expectation of objective probabilities is a passive representation of cognitive process and practice in which the nature of the habitus is inferred from the consequences of action. It raises awkward questions, such as: How do people know what the objective probabilities are? How, if not at the conscious level, do people act upon these perceptions of probability? Why, if actors can *see* 'the way things are', can they not go beyond this to *question* the way things are? How can an expectation be anything other than conscious? And so on. At best the formulation is vague, at worst it is an act of faith.

Thus, the habitus is the source of 'objective' practices, but is itself a set of 'subjective' generative principles produced by the 'objective' patterns of social life. Such a model is either another version of determination in the last instance, or a sophisticated form of functionalism. It is difficult to imagine a place in Bourdieu's scheme of things for his own emphasis upon the meaningful practices of social actors in their cultural context. One can only speculate as to how 'objective structures' are constituted or changed by that practice. Objective structures – whatever, for the moment, these might be – are somehow given as 'cultural arbitraries', which the actions of embodied agents then reproduce.[48]

Bourdieu's response to the accusation of determinism is three-fold.[49] First, he argues that the habitus only operates in relation to a social field. The same habitus can produce very different practices depending upon what is going on in the field. Second, the habitus can be transformed by changed circumstances, and expectations or aspirations will change with it. Third, the habitus can be controlled – and it is not clear what he means by this – as a result of the 'awakening of consciousness and socioanalysis'. Leaving the last point to one side, if only because I do not understand it, the first two rebuttals do not amount to a defence against the charge of determinism. Both depend on changed circumstances and it is not clear how these changes can be anything other than external to the social group concerned. It remains difficult to understand how, in Bourdieu's model of practice, actors or collectivities can intervene in their own history in any substantial fashion.

Finally, there is something more to be said about strategies and strategising. As an alternative to the idea that behaviour is rule-governed, the notion of strategising is an important link between the notions of practice, habitus and field. Strategies are, according to Bourdieu, the ongoing result of the interaction between the dispositions of the habitus and the constraints and possibilities which are the reality of any given social field – whether it be cultural consumption, landholding, education or whatever. Now the notion of strategy is not a new one in social science, nor is it in any sense straightforward. The various contributors to a recent debate about the use of the concept in sociology make a number of points which are of interest here.[50] First, there is agreement that the concept of strategy and strategising synthesises three elements: *rational calculation* tempered by *constraints*, particularly to do with resource allocation, oriented towards the achievement of objectives in the *medium to long term*. In this sense, the concept is offered as a contribution to the resolution of the 'structure/agency problem'. Second, there are other kinds of action than the strategic: the concept may be becoming overused, subsuming too much of what people do under the heading of rational calculation. Third, the notion of strategy in social science derives from its use in other fields, particularly war and business, where its importance is not so much in the rational achievement of stated goals as in its rhetorical capacity to give purpose and structure to collective action. Fourth, and bearing the previous point in mind, strategising may be a distinctively modern form of action, in contrast to various traditional forms of action.

In the light of this debate, Bourdieu's model of strategising, completely opposed as it is to conscious, calculative rational decision-making, is at odds with the concept's accepted meaning. One is forced to ask whether his is a justifiable use of the word, whether it does not serve to confuse rather than clarify matters.

The issues of calculation and decision-making, and conscious or unconscious process, are once again of central importance. If strategies are neither an aspect of conscious decision-making nor an 'unconscious program', as Bourdieu insists, one is entitled to ask just *what* they are and, with respect to the epistemological issues raised by empirical research, *how* one might identify them. In Bourdieu's case, the answer to the second question appears to be that strategies are recognisable by reference to the patterns of social practice which they are presumed to produce. In other words, as in structural functionalism, 'what goes on in people's heads' is confused or conflated with its putative consequences. In the case, for example, of Kabyle or Béarnais kinship and marriage patterns, since the 'official accounts' of ideal behaviour match up with so little of observed reality, another set of explanations – neither causes nor reasons – is produced, in the shape of unarticulated or inexplicit strategies, to explain what remains. Strategies, in Bourdieu's sense, are presumed to exist because, for explanatory purposes, they *must* exist. To use Bourdieu's own expression, we are slipping here from a model of reality to the reality of the model. Strategies appear to be more his creation than his research subjects'.

FIELD, MARKET AND CAPITAL

In a number of places in this chapter the expressions 'field' or 'social field' have been used with little or no explanation. In the course of an interview with Loic Wacquant, Bourdieu has provided us with a concise discussion of what he means by the metaphor and its place in his thinking.[51] A field, in Bourdieu's sense, is a social arena within which struggles or manoeuvres take place over specific resources or stakes and access to them. Fields are defined by the stakes which are at stake – cultural goods (life-style), housing, intellectual distinction (education), employment, land, power (politics), social class, prestige or whatever – and may be of differing degrees of specificity and concreteness. Each field, by virtue of its defining content, has a different logic and taken-for-granted structure of necessity and relevance which is both the product and producer of the habitus which is specific and appropriate to the field.

To think in terms of a field involves recognising the centrality of social relations to social analysis:

> I define a field as a network, or a configuration, of
> objective relations between positions objectively defined,
> in their existence and in the determinations they impose
> upon their occupants, agents or institutions, by their
> present and potential situation . . . in the structure of
> the distribution of power (or capital) whose possession
> commands access to the specific profits that are at stake
> in the field, as well as by their objective relation to other
> positions . . .[52]

A field, therefore, is a structured system of social positions –
occupied either by individuals or institutions – the nature of
which defines the situation for their occupants. It is also a system
of forces which exist between these positions; a field is structured
internally in terms of power relations. Positions stand in relationships of domination, subordination or equivalence (homology)
to each other by virtue of the access they afford to the goods or
resources (capital) which are at stake in the field. These goods
can be principally differentiated into four categories: economic
capital, social capital (various kinds of valued relations with significant others), cultural capital (primarily legitimate knowledge
of one kind or another) and symbolic capital (prestige and social
honour).[53] The nature of positions, their 'objective definition',
is to be found in their relationship to the relevant form of capital.
The existence of a field *presupposes* and, in its functioning,
creates a belief on the part of participants in the legitimacy and
value of the capital which is at stake in the field. This legitimate
interest in the field is produced by the same historical processes
which produce the field itself.[54]

Simple, preindustrial societies will have a relatively limited
number of effective fields. The more technologically complex
and socially differentiated the society, the more fields – 'relatively
autonomous social microcosms' – there will be. The boundaries
of fields are imprecise and shifting, determinable only by empirical research, although they include various institutionally constituted points of entry. The boundary of any given field, the
point(s) at which the field ceases to have any impact on practice,
is always at stake in the struggles which take place within the
field. A field is, by definition, 'a field of struggles' in which
agents' strategies are concerned with the preservation or
improvement of their positions with respect to the defining capital
of the field.

Using Bourdieu's concept of field in social research entails three distinct operations. First, the relationship of the field in question to the 'field of power' (politics) must be understood. The field of power is thus to be regarded as the dominant or preeminent field of any society; it is the source of the hierarchical power relations which structure all other fields. Second, within the field in question one must construct a 'social topology' or map of the 'objective structure' of the positions which make up the field, and the relationships between them in the competition for the field's specific form of capital. Third, the habitus(es) of the agents within the field must be analysed, along with the trajectories or strategies which are produced in the interaction between habitus and the constraints and opportunities which are determined by the structure of the field.

The field is the crucial mediating context wherein external factors – changing circumstances – are brought to bear upon individual practice and institutions. The logic, politics and structure of the field shape and channel the manner in which 'external determinations' affect what goes on within the field, making them appear a part of the ongoing history and operation of the field itself. The more important and autonomous the field in the context of the array of fields which together constitute a 'society', the more this metamorphosis effect operates.

Finally, Bourdieu argues that in the way in which they are organised or structured, and the manner in which they function or operate, there are many homologies between fields: 'each has its dominant and its dominated, its struggles for usurpation or exclusion, its mechanisms of reproduction, and so on. But every one of these characteristics takes on a specific, irreducible, form in each field . . .'[55] The homology between fields, the resemblance which is bound up with difference, has two sources. First, it is a reflection of certain commonalities of habitus and practice as they are translated within the differing logics of separate fields. Second, it is a consequence of the power of dominant fields, particularly the field of power (politics), to impinge upon weaker fields and structure what occurs within them. The weaker and less autonomous the field – Bourdieu's example is the 'philosophical field' – the more this 'overdetermination' can happen.

The use of the word 'capital' to describe the stakes in social fields alerts us to Bourdieu's appropriation of economic metaphor to understand social life. He has argued that his use of a language derived from economics does not leave him open to the charge of 'economism'.[56] In particular, in his use of a word such as 'interest', he stresses that, whereas for economists there is only one – universal – interest which dominates human endeavour, i.e. the pursuit of rational, material self-interest, narrowly defined, for him there are many interests. There are as many interests, as many values to be maximised, as there are fields. These interests are cultural or historical constructions, they are the objects of struggle, and can only be determined by empirical investigation. Economic rationality is only one such interest among many.

His defence in this case, would, I suspect, be accepted by an increasing number of institutional or radical economists. It is also an integral part of his rejection of rational action theories. However, there is confusion and contradiction in his thinking here. While accepting that interests are variable, it is very difficult to imagine how an 'interest' can be anything other than something which actors *consciously* pursue. The only alternative involves the detached social scientific observer deciding what actors' interests are – and hence what is in their interests. This is an approach which Bourdieu consistently rejects. Despite definitional protestations to the contrary, the use of the word 'interest' imports into the analysis either an unavoidable dimension of conscious, calculative decision-making or an indefensible epistemological conceit.

Similarly, his use of a market metaphor, as an alternative to the notion of the field, is revealing.[57] As arenas of struggle over valued stakes, fields are clearly regulated by a relationship between supply and demand. This allows the mobilisation of notions such as 'price' and 'cost' in relationship to the strategies or trajectories of agents engaged in competition within the field. The most conspicuous example of his use of the relationship between supply and demand is perhaps to be found in the study of the public use of art galleries,[58] but the metaphor of the marketplace is a consistent thread throughout his work. And the problem remains the same. It is difficult to reconcile the market model with Bourdieu's refusal to acknowledge that an appreciation of deliberate calculative action by individuals, informed by whatever rationale or values, has an important role to play in sociological or anthropological analyses.

Bourdieu's model of society – the 'social space', to adopt his own terminology – as consisting of inter-related fields is also important for his understanding of social collectivities, particularly social classes.[59] Classes, understood from an objectivist point of view, are categories of people who occupy positions within a field (the political field of power? the economic field?) which are, in terms of the topology of the field, similar or close to each other. The closer the positions are, the more likely is the participation of their occupants in a shared habitus, the possibility of their constitution as a social group through political struggle and the collective recognition of their identity as distinct from other groups or classes.[60] The social construction and classification of group identities – classes in this case – is one aspect of the struggles which characterise fields. This mobilisation, or movement from objectively defined classes to classes as subjectively constituted, is not inevitable, however, merely possible: 'Classes [for Bourdieu] . . . seem to have the epistemological status of tendencies which depend upon a series of factors, including conjunctural and voluntarist events, to determine whether they are actualised or not.'[61] For 'conjunctural' read 'external changed circumstances' and the problem is familiar and clear. We are back with the necessity for a *deus ex machina* if social change is to be rendered intelligible. This, of course, is inevitable given Bourdieu's attitude towards purposive, goal-oriented social action.

As a model of class society this also seems to owe more than a small debt to Marx's distinction between the class-in-itself (objectively defined) and the class-for-itself (subjective class consciousness). Bourdieu, however, with characteristic robustness and immodesty, disowns this formulation as a 'false solution' to the problems of class analysis.[62] It remains unclear, however – to this reader at least – how a false solution when it is offered by Marx becomes, when served up in only a slightly rehashed version by Bourdieu, somehow more palatable.

When one looks at how Bourdieu actually operationalises the concept of class in his empirical studies, such as *Reproduction* or *Distinction*, a further problem appears. In the first instance, classes are constituted in his work by the use of aggregate statistical data about individuals, classified according to formal occupational identity. This may be a tried and trusted convention of social stratification research, but it is also a strategy which either takes for granted or leaves up for grabs the substantive ontological status of classes as collectivities. It also imports into his research a somewhat impoverished understanding of class identity (as occupation) which is at odds with his attempts to understand social life in all of its complexity.

In this section, we have moved beyond individual behaviour (practice) and the collective social construction of the world (habitus) to discuss Bourdieu's model of 'social space' as constituted by the relationship between social fields, his equivalent of social structure or the macro-sociological level of analysis. As such it is an essential introduction to the discussions of cultural/ social reproduction and class culture(s) which follow in the next two chapters. Before leaving the topic, however, there are a number of comments or criticisms to be made.

In the first place, as a model of 'social structure' it is not particularly novel. From Weber onwards, the history of social theory is full of examples of broadly similar understandings of society as inter-related arenas or domains. This would not even be a comment worth making if Bourdieu did not persist in presenting his work as consisting of new and radical solutions to the old theoretical problems which have persistently stumped everyone else.

Of more weight is the suggestion that there is a problem either of ontology or definition (or both) with respect to fields. Do they exist in the social consciousness of those actors who inhabit the social space in question, or are they simply analytical constructs? It is not wholly clear. If the latter, how are they to be delineated or defined? This question is related to the first and is not clear either. The limits or boundaries of a field are a matter for empirical investigation, says Bourdieu, suggesting that they are a social as well as an analytical or theorised construct. However, what he does *not* tell us, even in response to a direct question,[63] is how the existence of a field is to be determined or how fields are to be identified.

Third, his writings on this subject reveal a central problem of Bourdieu's general sociology: there is little to be found in the way of a theorised model of institutions, their operation or their relationship to the organisation of social life. They seem to exist as taken for granted, functioning entities with a status similar to individual actors. This can be seen in the quotation at footnote[52] above: it is 'agents or institutions' which occupy the positions of the field. Although Bourdieu does discuss the 'codification' of culture and although he has written extended empirical analyses of the French education system, he does not take seriously enough the difference between people and institutions.

Nor does he move beyond a 'black box' model of institutions to understand what might be going on within them. He says something about their general procedures and structures, and the agendas which their functioning presumes, but little more. Nor does he say enough about the institutionalised nature of fields. There is in Bourdieu's social theory a gap, which is only partly filled by the notion of the habitus, between the micro level of practising agents and the macro level of fields and the social space. A theoretical model of institutions is required to fill this gap.

This comment may be related to the next criticism: the relationship between habitus and field is far from clear. In places, he writes as if each field generates its own specific habitus. Elsewhere, it seems to be the case that actors bring to whichever field they are a part of their own, preexisting and historically constituted habituses. Both of these options may, of course, be true. Individuals must grow up, acquiring their habitus as part of their process of social and personal development, within a field or fields. But what about fields which agents only ever encounter as mature, formed adults? And how, if at all, is it possible for a field to 'have' its own habitus, if the habitus is a property of embodied, individual agents? Once again we are back to problems of ontology and definition.

Finally, to return to the suggestion that there is more than a passing similarity between Bourdieu's theory and structural functionalism, his model of field(s) and social space is essentially one of equilibrium and stability. Social change is peripheral to the model and difficult to account for. There are a number of ways in which this point can be made. The centrality in his work of 'external determinations' as the motor force of change suggests an inability to account or allow for endogenous or internally generated change. The 'objective structures' of fields appear to be as durable as the dispositions of the habitus. The use of the market metaphor is another example of the same problem. It implies the operation of mechanisms which serve perpetually to re-establish equilibrium within the system.

Bourdieu's model is one in which power and authority flow from the top down. Despite his apparent acknowledgement of, and enthusiasm for, resistance, it is difficult to find examples in his work of its efficacy or importance. The ongoing and successful reproduction of relationships of domination lies at the heart of Bourdieu's social theory: there may be struggle, but it occurs within an enduringly hierarchical social space. While this state of affairs might come *close* to being the norm of historical experience, it is flouted sufficiently often to render the explanation of disruption and change of vital significance. Bourdieu's social theory does not enable us to do this, other than by resort to factors which impinge on the social arena in question from outside. His social universe ultimately remains one in which things happen to people, rather than a world in which they can intervene in their individual and collective destinies.

ONTOLOGY, EPISTEMOLOGY AND THEORY

The yardstick against which Bourdieu's theory must be assessed is his own goal of transcending the objectivist/subjectivist divide in the hope of constructing a sociology which adequately 'bridges the gap' between individual agency and social structure. By these criteria his project is a failure, albeit an impressive and interesting failure.

One root of the problem is that he remains trapped within an objectivist point of view. Thompson has recently put it like this: 'Bourdieu's view is that both subjectivism and objectivism are inadequate intellectual orientations, but that the latter is less inadequate than the former.'[64] I want to go further than this: Bourdieu cannot hope to achieve his theoretical aims without letting go of *both* ends of the dualism, and this he fails to do. In his sociological heart of hearts he is as committed to an objectivist view of the world as the majority of those whose work he so sternly dismisses.

The fact that he continues to use the words 'objective' and 'subjective' to denote different kinds of social facts or social reality, and 'objectivism' and 'subjectivism' to denote different ways of knowing – or modes of explaining – the world, is both revealing and confusing. It is revealing of an inability to either move beyond the dualism he claims to detest or think in terms other than those which are rooted in that dualism. It is confusing because (a) it conflates issues to do with the constitution of the social world as an object of study (ontology) with the way in which we know or explain it (epistemology), and (b) this conflation – the use of similar words to carry meanings which are actually different – allows him to mask or overlook contradictions between ontology and epistemology which go some way towards undermining his project from within.

In his sociological constitution of a universe to be analysed –
the social world – his approach can be described as *empiricist*.[65]
This is an essentially materialist viewpoint of social reality as
a set of inter-related physical phenomena: individual people,
observable events and tangible things. In a word, this is an
objective world:

> The proper object of social science, then, is neither indi-
> viduals . . . nor groups as sets of concrete individuals
> sharing a similar location in social space, but the *relation
> between two realizations of historical action*, in bodies (or
> biological individuals) and in things.[66]

This suggests a distrust of anything other than the 'real' world
of the visible. As a consequence, there is uncertainty or ambiguity about the status of elements of social life which have tra-
ditionally been the mainstay of sociological analysis. Take, for
example, social groups. They do not actually figure much in his
work. Ethnicity is something which he rarely considers, except
in his early research in North Africa, where he takes for granted
the existence and group boundaries of the Kabyles, the Sharvia,
the Mozabites, etc., as things which do not require explanation.
In his discussion of social classes he tends towards formalism and
statistical individualism, taking their nature and existence as
given (although, insofar as he does consider class formation as
a social process, this is a limited exception to my criticism).
Social identity, where he mentions it, is either seen from a
strictly individualistic standpoint,[67] or as a construct of ritual or
intellectual specialists.[68] His enthusiasm for statistics – aggregate data about individuals – and his fondness for the market
metaphor, with its implicit basis in individual behaviour, further
emphasise the individualism of his ontological world-view
(despite his protestations to the contrary). Bourdieu offers us
no theorised understanding of social groups or social (group)
identity.

Culture is another problem, for similar reasons. It appears in
his work as either an assemblage of consumable, material artifacts – everything from pop records to children's clothes to paint-
ings – or as an abstract, rhetorical concept, which occupies the
realm of the unconscious. Either way it does not do much
explanatory work. The concept of the habitus – *embodied* dispositions – functions as an analogue for culture when it comes to
explaining behaviour. But what does embodiment *mean* in this

context, other than a gesture of faith in the direction of materiality (as in '*biological* individuals')? What exactly *is* the habitus? How does it relate to the notion of 'culture'? How can individuals, social classes (groups) and fields all, in some way, 'have' distinctive and characteristic habituses? The criterion of embodiment makes habitus a reasonable enough individualistic concept – allowing for its problems of definition – but a wholly implausible attribute of collective or abstract social entities.

This is intimately related to a further difficulty in Bourdieu's work. Any theory of human social practice must, of necessity, entail a philosophy or theory of the mind, whether this be implicit or explicit.[69] Three central problems in the philosophy of the mind are of relevance here: the relationship between the mind and the body; the relationship between thought and action; and the relationship between conscious and unconscious mental processes.

Bourdieu's solution to the first problem is certainly novel: he projects the mind onto (not into) the body, which is then treated as a mnemonic device. Mind, if you like, becomes an epiphenomenon, almost an *effect*, of the body. With respect to the second, he simply dismisses thinking – understood as a conscious process of deliberation – by denying its significance. The third case is more interesting: having dismissed conscious thought, his empiricism leaves him similarly sceptical about the existence or knowability of the invisible unconscious. His way out of this dilemma, the habitus, exists somewhere between the two states, a sub-mind of embodied habituation and thoughtless practice which could easily have its theoretical origins in behaviourist psychology.[70] We still do not know *what* the habitus is or *how* it works to generate practices, an ignorance which is only compounded by the fact that its existence can only be inferred from its putative practical effects. Bourdieu is revealed as working with an impoverished, two-dimensional model of individuals and agency.

Lastly, there is an ontological weakness which we have already discussed: what is a 'field' (and, by implication, what is the 'social space')? In order to avoid concepts such as 'social structure' – the sociological invisible of invisibles – some such notion is almost inevitable if the social landscape is to be adequately constituted for sociological purposes. Yet its ontological status remains unclear: is it 'real', is it a common-sensical category, or is it purely an analytical concept? This lack of clarity comes into focus if we consider the constituent components of fields, 'objectively defined positions', and some of the entities which occupy them, specifically institutions, which Bourdieu presents as somehow equivalent to agents (biological individuals again). This simply will not do. If we do adopt a point of view in which actors as individuals are the basic unit of sociological analysis, this does not excuse a neglect of institutional analysis, as the example of Weber makes clear. This absence is a direct result of Bourdieu's inability to constitute institutions as sociologically appropriate ontological constructions.

So, at the ontological level, in the constitution by the observer of the social world as a 'reality' which is available for study and analysis, there are two problems in Bourdieu's writings. Both derive from the adoption of an essentially distrustful empiricism. First, his social space is inhabited by a very limited range of definite phenomena: biological individuals, observable events and material things. Everything else is uncertain and ambiguous. Second, of these, his model of individual agents is woefully unconvincing and thin.

Coming to Bourdieu's epistemology – how he knows reality and, hence, his mode of explaining it – things look rather different, however. It is a form of *realism* which we can call *substantialism*. Realism is the view that reality lies somewhere beyond or behind the obvious world of appearances. Substantialism says that 'the social world is conceived as an objective material structure of relations. This structure is not accessible to direct observation. In fact, what *can* be observed must, in turn, be explained by that underlying structure of material relations.'[71] Although empiricism and substantialism are both forms of materialism, they are mutually exclusive. The ambiguities and difficulties of definition and ontology which are outlined above result from the muddled interaction of the two in Bourdieu's thinking. The habitus, for example, is both an empirical/material phenomenon, in its embodiment, and, as an explanation of practice, something which exists beyond the realm of appearances. It becomes neither fowl nor fish. The contradiction between empiricism and substantialism hides behind the notion of the 'objective' and its analogue, 'objectivity'. Both are based on a model of an objective or real world, and both are modalities of objectivism, but in each case the word 'objective' means rather different things. The result is confusion.

Bourdieu's theory of practice illustrates the problem. The

reality of practice, what people do, is typically established either through direct observation of behaviour or by recourse to statistics (both positivistic approaches). However, its explanation has to be sought somewhere else. The actors' own explanations of their practice are (a) no more than another practice, part of the world of empirical reality, and hence (b) from a realist perspective, either insufficient or unreliable. They are, rather, something to be explained. While the reality to be explained consists solely of individuals and things and the relations between them, 'what is really going on' ('real' reality) is more than or different to that empirical universe. As a result, despite his rejection of the epistemological arrogance of structuralism, where the social scientist (like mother) knows best, he eventually adopts a similar position. Actors may believe that they act, at least in part, by formulating goals, making decisions and putting them into effect. They may, what is more, explain this to the inquiring sociologist. Bourdieu, however, knows that this is an illusion; the true explanation of behaviour is to be found in the habitus.

It is not just actors' accounts which become problematic. As a result of his impoverished view of empirical social reality, the 'real' substance of the social world, the things which can explain empirical fact, must be constructed in a shadowy world, beyond the visible yet somehow 'objective'. Hence the problematic status and definition of habitus, group, institution and field. They are ambiguous analytical creations operating, of necessity, behind actors' backs. Hence also the confusion which sometimes emerges in Bourdieu's work with respect to whether the categories he deploys are common-sense or analytical concepts.

It may be possible to relate this problem to Bourdieu's 'epistemological experimentation' and the 'objectification of objectification'. The detachment from social reality which is required by objectification, is, in Bourdieu's case, simply the constitution of that social reality as *objective*: this is his empiricism. What is entailed in stepping back one further step – the 'epistemological break' which problematises that initial constitution of objectivity – may be a commitment to realism which, in conjunction with Bourdieu's materialism, produces a substantialist approach.

This confusion surfaces in Bourdieu's substantive theory. His theory of practice is surprisingly – because, after all, this is what practice is supposed to be about – deficient, at all levels, in its conceptualisation of *process*. As Connell has observed, where there should be a specification of process, there is a 'black box',[72] a criticism which is broadly analogous to Elster's identification of an absence of a causal 'mechanism' in Bourdieu's work.[73]

This absence is conspicuous when we look at cognition and mental processes. However, much the same can also be said at the other extreme of social reality, with respect to institutions and social structure (regardless, for the moment, of how the latter is defined). The closest we get to a model of process here is an individualistic, and hence, paradoxically, somewhat abstract, model of 'struggle', albeit a struggle that is typically doomed to merely reproducing the constraints against which it is pitted. The absence of a processual element, whether of the micro or macro variety, derives from the problematic juxtaposition of empiricism and substantialism in which Bourdieu's theory is grounded.

It is not, however, that process is wholly absent. Where it does exist it is largely concerned with the visible world of what Bourdieu has described, in an appreciation of Erving Goffman, as the 'infinitely small': walking, standing, modes of speech, the things that are summarised in the concept of bodily hexis. Beyond this, in the middle range which is so important to sociology, there is a theoretical gap in which actors' strategies are both identified *and* explained by reference to their supposed outcomes. The 'how?' question of processual analysis is answered in strictly empirical terms, by reference to a sequence of events. The 'why?' question is only ever answered with benefit of hindsight.

Here is also revealed Bourdieu's limited understanding of history as little more than the cumulation of one thing following another. This is history as narrative and biography. Process is repetitive and uniform – the mundane universals of how people do things. With respect to social practice and history there is little attempt to develop a theorised model of *why* people do things, or *why* things are the way they are, that is in any sense dynamic in the medium to long term. Process and history are *described* rather than *understood*. Social change, for example, may be the product of the 'external determination' of changed circumstances, but *why* have those circumstances changed?

What this suggests is that the charge of determinism is, in Bourdieu's case, justified. In the 'subjective expectation of objective probability', the appearance of meaningful practice is actually the reality of a self-fulfilling prophecy. Social structure and history produce the habitus. This, in turn, generates practices which serve, in the absence of external factors, to reproduce social structure. As a consequence, history tends to repeat itself.

A similar sequence or pattern prevails in the lives of individuals. If ever there was an 'oversocialised conception of man' – to appropriate Dennis Wrong's indictment of structural functionalism [74] – it is Pierre Bourdieu's. Any substantial deviance from the imperatives of the habitus is so inconceivable that he does not even consider it. His model of practice, despite all of its references to improvisation and fluidity, turns out to be a celebration of (literally) mindless conformity.

At the end of the day, perhaps the most crucial weakness in Bourdieu's work is his inability to cope with subjectivity. There are two aspects of this problem which deserve emphasis. First, actors are more knowledgeable about the social world than Bourdieu is prepared to allow. To suggest this may appear unfair, given that his theory insists that people do know the 'objective probabilities' which govern their lives. This, however, is a strange form of knowledge, neither conscious nor unconscious, largely unidentifiable except inasmuch as it is analytically necessary in order to explain their behaviour. Even curiouser, it turns out to be a form of *collective* unconscious knowledge, about the life chances of *categories* of actors, although it forms the basis of *individual* practices. What is more, it is only accurate up to a point, when it becomes a form of false knowledge (about which more will be said in Chapter Five). Actors *must* know more about their situation, and that knowledge must be more valid, than Bourdieu proposes.

Second, and it is by now a familiar argument, the role in social life of deliberate, knowing, decision-making, informed by whatever rationality is the order of the day, is vastly underestimated by Bourdieu. To say this is not to insist that it is the *only* process guiding or generating behaviour, merely to argue for its appreciation as a significant dimension of practice. Bourdieu's refusal to accept this leads him inexorably into deterministic explanations. Despite the significance which he attaches to the temporality of practice, his theory becomes a machine for the suppression of history, banishing it with an eternal ethnographic present that is indistinguishable from the past and prefigures the future. It is a world where behaviour has its causes, but actors are not allowed their reasons.

It would be more than unjust to end this chapter on such a negative note. It must, for example, be acknowledged that, inasmuch as Bourdieu's theory of practice is labyrinthine in both form and content, there are available alternative, and more positive, readings of his work.[75] The interested reader should look at these as well as the original texts. Nor does my critique detract from my earlier argument about Bourdieu being 'good to think with'. His work is demanding, thoughtful and ambitious in an area of social theory which is of strategic importance both to the overall sociological and anthropological project of understanding society and social relations between human beings and to the more specific theoretical project of understanding the relationship between the historical pattern of social relations (structure) and mundane social interaction by real people (agency). His difficulties can teach us much.

To leave it at that, however, would be to risk the charge of consigning Bourdieu to damnation by faint praise. Such is not my intention. He offers useful and suggestive insights into how socially competent behaviour is achieved, although his notion of 'excellence' is problematic. His argument that social practice is not rule *governed* is well taken, although he underestimates the importance of rules as *one* resource which contributes to the overall mix of freedom and constraint which characterises behaviour. Similarly, his emphasis upon the improvisatory character of practice is clearly correct. So is his identification of the thoughtlessness of habit as a factor enabling individuals to go about their daily lives without having to consider every move they make (although, in this latter case, he seems to add little to earlier, less obscure discussions of habituation[76]). Further, while it is somewhat muddled, his proposal that key areas of culture are embodied, rather than simply 'in the mind', is both challenging and original. All the more reason for the further clarification and refinement which it appears to demand.

Moving away from the pragmatics of practice, his argument about the way in which people collude in their own domination, while overstated and deterministic (and, once again, not particularly novel), resonates with a complex and substantial plausibility. Control, censorship and conformism are never more effective than when they are self-imposed. Each in their own way, Marx, Weber and Durkheim all understood this. So does Bourdieu. In the next chapter, I will explore his understanding of the processes which lead us into this collusion as they are revealed in his studies of education.

NOTES AND REFERENCES

[1] M. Hollis, *Models of Man*, Cambridge, Cambridge University Press (1977), p. 12.
[2] J.B. Thompson, 'Editor's Introduction' to P. Bourdieu, *Language and Symbolic Power*, Cambridge, Polity (1991), p. 11.
[3] The best known contributor to this debate is Anthony Giddens; see his *New Rules of the Sociological Method*, London, Hutchinson (1976), and *The Constitution of Society*, Cambridge, Polity (1984). For a flavour of the arguments, see D. Held and J.B. Thompson (eds), *Social Theory of Modern Societies: Anthony Giddens and his Critics*, Cambridge, Cambridge University Press (1989). For an impressive alternative to Giddens, see M.S. Archer, *Culture and Agency: The Place of Culture in Social Theory*, Cambridge, Cambridge University Press (1988), a work which also has interesting things to say about Bourdieu. For a comparison of Bourdieu and Giddens, see: R. Jenkins, 'Pierre Bourdieu and the Reproduction of Determinism', *Sociology*, vol. 16 (1982), pp. 270–81.
[4] L.D. Wacquant, 'Towards a Reflexive Sociology: A Workshop with Pierre Bourdieu', *Sociological Theory*, vol. 7 (1989), p. 50.
[5] P. Bourdieu, *Outline of a Theory of Practice*, Cambridge, Cambridge University Press (1977), pp. 10, 96; *In Other Words*, Cambridge, Polity Press (1990), p. 13.
[6] T.B. Bottomore and M. Rubel (eds), *Karl Marx: Selected Writings in Sociology and Social Philosophy*, Harmondsworth, Pelican (1963), p. 84. The quotation is Thesis VIII.
[7] P. Bourdieu, *In Other Words*, op. cit., p. 13.
[8] P. Bourdieu, *Outline of a Theory . . .*, op. cit., pp. 96–7.
[9] *Ibid.*, p. 8.
[10] P. Bourdieu, *In Other Words*, op. cit., p. 61.
[11] E. Goffman, *The Presentation of Self in Everyday Life*, Harmondsworth, Pelican (1971; first published 1959); *Encounters*, Indianapolis, Bobbs-Merrill (1961); *Strategic Interaction*, Oxford, Basil Blackwell (1970). See Bourdieu's tribute on Goffman's death: 'Erving Goffman, Discoverer

of the Infinitely Small', *Theory, Culture and Society*, vol. 2 (1983), pp. 112–13.

[12] L.D. Wacquant, 'Towards a reflexive sociology', *op. cit.*, p. 42.

[13] P. Bourdieu, *Language and Symbolic Power*, *op. cit.*, p. 235. The reader who consults this passage will see a further explicit acknowledgement to the work of Goffman.

[14] P. Bourdieu, *The Logic of Practice*, Cambridge, Polity (1990), p. 20.

[15] P. Bourdieu, *Outline of a Theory . . .*, *op. cit.*, p. 8.

[16] *Ibid.*, pp. 29, 73.

[17] P. Bourdieu, *In Other Words*, *op. cit.*, p. 60.

[18] P. Bourdieu, *The Logic of Practice*, *op. cit.*, pp. 98–111.

[19] *Ibid.*, pp. 147–61.

[20] *Ibid.*, pp. 162–99.

[21] P. Bourdieu, *In Other Words*, *op. cit.*, pp. 62–3.

[22] *Ibid.*, p. 66.

[23] See, for example, J. Elster, *Nuts and Bolts for the Social Scientist*, Cambridge, Cambridge University Press (1989). Bourdieu's critique of Elster's work – about which he uses epithets such as 'mediocre' – can be found in: *The Logic of Practice*, *op. cit.*, pp. 46–51; L.D. Wacquant, 'Towards a Reflexive Sociology', *op. cit.*, pp. 43–5.

[24] L.D. Wacquant, 'Towards a Reflexive Sociology', *op. cit.*, pp. 43–4.

[25] There is, of course, a contradiction here between this criticism of rational action theory, and Bourdieu's critique of its propensity to substitute arbitrary analytical models for social reality.

[26] P. Bourdieu, *In Other Words*, *op. cit.*, p. 8.

[27] E. Panofsky, *Architecture gothique et pensée scholastique*, tr. P. Bourdieu, Paris, Éditions de Minuit (1967).

[28] P. Bourdieu, *In Other Words*, *op. cit.*, p. 12.

[29] P. Bourdieu, *Outline of a Theory . . .*, *op. cit.*, p. 95.

[30] P. Bourdieu, *The Logic of Practice*, *op. cit.*, pp. 66–79.

[31] P. Bourdieu, *Outline of a Theory . . .*, *op. cit.*, p. 87.

[32] *Ibid.*, pp. 93, 94.

[33] See, for example, D. Robbins, *The Work of Pierre Bourdieu*, Buckingham, Open University Press (1991), p. 204, n. 23.

[34] P. Bourdieu, *Outline of a Theory . . .*, p. 214, n. 1.

[35] *Ibid.*, p. 79.

[36] L.D. Wacquant, 'Towards a Reflexive Sociology', *op. cit.*, p. 45.

[37] P. Bourdieu, *The Logic of Practice*, *op. cit.*, pp. 52–65; *Language and Symbolic Power*, *op. cit.*, pp. 37–42.

[38] Bourdieu has described this process of translation and transposition as 'irresistable analogy': *The Logic of Practice*, *op. cit.*, pp. 200–270.

[39] P. Bourdieu, *Distinction: A Social Critique of the Judgement of Taste*, London, Routledge and Kegan Paul (1984), pp. 172–3.

[40] See J. Lyons, *Chomsky*, London, Fontana (1970).

[41] P. Bourdieu and J.-C. Passeron, *Reproduction in Education, Society and Culture*, London, Sage (1977), p. 205.

[42] P. Bourdieu, *Outline of a Theory . . .*, *op. cit.*, p. 83.

[43] *Ibid.*, p. 54.

[44] P. Bourdieu, *The Logic of Practice*, *op. cit.*, p. 53.

[45] *Ibid.*, p. 54.

[46] *Ibid.*, p. 59.

[47] J. Elster, *Sour Grapes: Studies in the Subversion of Rationality*, Cambridge, Cambridge University Press (1983), pp. 69–71, 101–8.

[48] P. Bourdieu and J.-C. Passeron, *Reproduction*, *op. cit.*, p. 23.

[49] P. Bourdieu, *In Other Words*, *op. cit.*, p. 116.

[50] This debate, with contributions from Crow, Morgan, Shaw, Knight and Morgan, and Watson, can be found in *Sociology*, vol. 23 (1989) no. 1 and vol. 24 (1990) no. 3.

[51] L.D. Wacquant, 'Towards a Reflexive Sociology', *op. cit.*, pp. 37–41.

[52] *Ibid.*, p. 39.

[53] P. Bourdieu, *Language and Symbolic Power*, *op. cit.*, pp. 229–31.

[54] P. Bourdieu, *In Other Words*, *op. cit.*, p. 88.

[55] L.D. Wacquant, 'Towards a Reflexive Sociology', *op. cit.*, p. 41.

[56] *Ibid.*, pp. 41–2; P. Bourdieu, *In Other Words*, *op. cit.*, pp. 87–93.

[57] See, for example, P. Bourdieu, *Language and Symbolic Power*, *op. cit.*, pp. 66–89.

[58] P. Bourdieu and A. Darbel, with D. Schnapper, *The Love of Art: European Art Museums and their Public*, Cambridge, Polity (1991).

[59] See the chapter by Wilkes in R. Harker, C. Maher and C. Wilkes (eds), *An Introduction to the Work of Pierre Bourdieu*, London, Macmillan (1990), pp. 109–31.

[60] P. Bourdieu, *Language and Symbolic Power*, op. cit., pp. 229–51.

[61] C. Wilkes, in Harker *et al.*, *An Introduction* . . ., op. cit., p. 114.

[62] *Ibid.*, p. 112.

[63] L.D. Wacquant, 'Towards a Reflexive Sociology', op. cit., p. 39.

[64] J.B. Thompson, 'Editor's Introduction', op. cit., p. 11.

[65] Here, and in what follows, I draw heavily upon the excellent discussion of the relationship between ontology, epistemology and theory in: T. Johnson, C. Dandeker and C. Ashworth, *The Structure of Social Theory*, London, Macmillan (1984).

[66] L.D. Wacquant, 'Towards a Reflexive Sociology', op. cit., p. 44.

[67] P. Bourdieu, *Language and Symbolic Power*, op. cit., p. 235.

[68] *Ibid.*, pp. 117–26, 220–8.

[69] Useful introductions to the philosophy of the mind are: P. Carruthers, *Introducing Persons*, London, Croom Helm (1986); S. Priest, *Theories of the Mind*, London, Penguin (1991); S. Shoemaker and R. Swinburne, *Personal Identity*, Oxford, Basil Blackwell (1984).

[70] A similar point has been made by R.W. Connell, *Which Way Is Up?*, Sydney, George Allen and Unwin Australia (1983) pp. 151–3.

[71] T. Johnson *et al.*, *The Structure of Social Theory*, op.cit., p. 21.

[72] R.W. Connell, *Which Way Is Up?*, op. cit., p. 151.

[73] J. Elster, *Sour Grapes*, op. cit., p. 106.

[74] D. Wrong, 'The Oversocialised Conception of Man in Modern Sociology', *American Sociological Review*, vol. 26 (1961), pp. 183–93.

[75] R. Harker *et al.*, *An Introduction* . . ., op. cit., pp. 1–25; D. Robbins, *The Work of Pierre Bourdieu*, op. cit., pp. 102–16.

[76] P.L. Berger and T. Luckmann, *The Social Construction of Reality*, London, Allen Lane (1967), pp. 70–85.

5

Symbolic Violence and Social Reproduction

Bourdieu's sociology of education is likely to be the aspect of his work with which most readers are familiar. Rather than simply as a contribution to a specialist area of sociology, this aspect of Bourdieu's writing and research is best understood as an extension of his theory of practice to construct a general 'theory of symbolic violence', on the one hand, and an equally general theory of the social reproduction of advanced industrial societies, on the other. It can also profitably be read as the focused application to a particular field – education – of the theoretical framework outlined in the previous chapter.

In this chapter I will first summarise the basic propositions of Bourdieu's theory of symbolic violence. This will be followed by a discussion of his best-known studies of the relationship between education and social reproduction. The final section will deal briefly with Bourdieu's model of the processes whereby the French system of higher education reproduces itself.

SYMBOLIC VIOLENCE

In constructing a 'theory of symbolic violence', Bourdieu and Passeron attempt to specify in theoretical terms the processes whereby, in all societies, order and social restraint are produced by indirect, cultural mechanisms rather than by direct, coercive social control. In doing so, they draw heavily upon Weber, in particular upon his discussions of authority and legitimate domination.[1] Although nominally the product of two authors, the style and content are so much of a piece with the rest of Bourdieu's work (similar problems are dealt with, for example, in Book One, Chapter Eight, of *The Logic of Practice*) that I will discuss it here as though it were written by only one hand. I will treat his other collaborations with Passeron in the same way. The ideas are very clearly Bourdieu's (as is the language).

The theory of symbolic violence is systematically laid out in the first half of *Reproduction in Education, Society and Culture*, first published in French in 1970.[2] Written in language which has been described as 'truly remarkably obscure and abstract',[3] the theory – or, rather, to be fair to Bourdieu's own characterisation of it, the *foundations* of the theory – is presented as a series of cumulative propositions and glosses, a stylistic device which further undermines its readability. The theory was developed in the course of empirical research on the French education system, but it obviously draws upon Bourdieu's Algerian work and is intended to 'apply to any social formation, understood as a system of power relations and sense relations between groups or classes'.[4] In outlining it here, I have attempted to render the theory as accessible as possible while at the same time remaining true to the language in which the original is couched.

Symbolic violence, according to Bourdieu, is the imposition of systems of symbolism and meaning (i.e. culture) upon groups or classes in such a way that they are experienced as legitimate. This legitimacy obscures the power relations which permit that imposition to be successful. Insofar as it is accepted as legitimate, culture adds its own force to those power relations, contributing to their systematic reproduction. This is achieved through a process of *misrecognition*: 'the process whereby power relations are perceived not for what they objectively are but in a form which renders them legitimate in the eyes of the beholder'.[5] Culture is arbitrary in two senses, in its imposition and in its content.

What the notion of arbitrariness denotes here is that, other than as the result of an empirically traceable history, culture cannot be deduced or derived from any notions of appropriateness or relative value. All cultures are equally arbitrary – this is an implied critique of the notion of 'culture with a capital C' – and, in the final analysis, behind all culture lies the arbitrary sanction of 'pure de facto power'.[6] This is what Bourdieu means when he talks of the 'cultural arbitrary'.

The mainstay of the exercise of symbolic violence is 'pedagogic action', the imposition of a cultural arbitrary, of which there are three modes: *diffuse education*, which occurs in the course of interaction with competent members of the social formation in question (an example might be the informal peer group), *family education*, which speaks for itself, and *institutionalised education* (examples of which might be age-set initiation rituals, on the one hand, or school, on the other). The symbolic strength of any pedagogic agency – its capacity successfully to inculcate meaning – is a function of its 'weight' in the structure of power relations.

Pedagogic action, in reproducing culture in all its arbitrariness, also reproduces the power relations which underwrite its own operation. This is 'the social reproduction function of cultural reproduction'.[7] Pedagogic actions reflect the interests of dominant groups or classes, tending to reproduce the uneven distribution of cultural capital among the groups or classes which inhabit the social space in question, hence reproducing social structure. Pedagogic action involves the exclusion of ideas as unthinkable, as well as their positive inculcation (depending, of course, upon the nature of the ideas). Exclusion or censorship may in fact be the most effective mode of pedagogic action.

'Pedagogic authority' is a necessary component or condition of successful pedagogic action. It is an arbitrary power to act, misrecognised by its practitioners and recipients as legitimate. This legitimacy makes it possible for pedagogic action to work. It is experienced as neutral, or even positively valued, but no pedagogic action is actually neutral or 'culturally free'. Pedagogic authority is so fundamental that it is often implicitly or explicitly identified with the 'natural' or 'primordial' relationship between parent and child. Although technical competence may be an aspect of the explicit claim to educational legitimacy, it is actually a matter of institutional authority. Every agency exerting pedagogic action is authoritative (legitimate) only inasmuch as it is a 'mandated representative' of the group whose cultural arbitrary it imposes. Pedagogic authority is bestowed, not earned.

This authority is not uniform within or between all groups and classes. Ideas, says Bourdieu, have effects which are most strong when they encounter and reinforce preexisting dispositions (his example being the somewhat gnomic utterance that 'the prophet always preaches to the converted'). What this means is that the differing success of pedagogic action in different groups or classes is, in the first place, a function of the fact that each group or class has a different 'pedagogic ethos'. By this he means a disposition towards pedagogy (education) which is a consequence of family education and a recognition of the likely market or material value of education to members of the class or group. In the latter, we have the re-appearance of the 'subjective expectation of objective probability'. Pedagogic authority becomes more legitimate when the sanctions which it has at its disposal are confirmed, for any given collectivity, by the market in which the value of the products of the pedagogic action concerned is determined. For example (my own this time), the legitimacy of education for working-class pupils largely depends, shall we say, on the trade-in value of formal credentials in the labour market. In a time of high unemployment, this legitimacy, this pedagogic authority, is likely to come under pressure.

Pedagogic action is achieved by 'pedagogic work':

> a process of inculcation which must last long enough to produce a durable training, i.e. a *habitus*, the product of internalization of the principles of a cultural arbitrary capable of perpetuating itself after PA [pedagogic action] has ceased and thereby of perpetuating in practices the principles of the internalized arbitrary.[8]

As an aside here, we may note that Bourdieu is apparently mobilising a subtly different model of the habitus to the one which was outlined in Chapter Four. The emphasis here on pedagogy/education, on a 'process of inculcation' which he describes as 'training', would seem to suggest that explicit teaching is more important than implicit experience in the internalisation of the habitus. Because of the importance of pedagogic work, pedagogic action takes time and requires consistency, distinguishing it from other forms of symbolic violence (such as, once again, the preaching of the prophet). Pedagogic agencies are also, therefore, of longer duration and greater stability than other agencies of symbolic violence.

The long-term function or effect of pedagogic work is, at least in part, the production of dispositions which generate 'correct' responses to the symbolic stimuli emanating from agencies endowed with pedagogic authority. Thus, in adult life, preaching reactivates the memory and experience of the childhood Christian upbringing. Pedagogic work, and its results, are a substitute for physical constraint and coercion; it is produced out of or by pedagogic authority and subsequently reinforces it. Bourdieu argues that the experience – as a pupil – of pedagogic work is the objective condition which generates the misrecognition of culture as arbitrary and bestows upon it the taken-for-granted quality of naturalness. Pedagogic work legitimates its product by producing legitimate consumers of that product (be it symbolised by formal credentials or the scarification of initiation).

The more pedagogic work is done, the more it tends to obscure 'the objective truth of the habitus as the internalization of the principles of a cultural arbitrary',[9] an internalisation which proceeds apace with the process of inculcation. Pedagogic work has the function of 'keeping order' by this means, through linked processes of self-limitation and self-censorship. The legitimate culture becomes experienced as an axiom, a *fait accompli*: children all too soon stop asking 'Why?'. Exclusion works most powerfully as self-exclusion.

This learning, this process of inculcation, is effectively irreversible (dispositions are 'durable'). It is, what is more, cumulative: the habitus acquired during family education is the basis for the receipt of the classroom message, which, in its turn, is the basis for the response to all subsequent cultural and intellectual messages. The early years of life remain, however, the most important.

Any specific 'mode of inculcation' – the systematic means by which pedagogic work is achieved – can be classified on a continuum from the *implicit* to the *explicit*. The first is 'the unconscious inculcation of principles which manifest themselves only in their practical state', the second is 'methodically organized' and inculcates 'articulated and even formalized principles (explicit pedagogy)'.[10] The difference between them is not relative efficiency; it is, rather, in their nature and content. Implicit pedagogy is best suited to 'traditional' or 'total' knowledge – which Bourdieu exemplifies as the 'assimilation of styles or knacks' – insofar as it is transmitted through close personal contact between master and apprentice or disciple. By strong implication, explicit pedagogy is most at home with 'modern', 'rational' or 'specialised' knowledge.

This distinction is relevant for class differences. Dominant or elite groups are distanced from the practical material demands of need which 'thrust a pragmatic disposition on the dominated class'.[11] As a consequence they will be dispositionally better placed to harmonise with, and take the maximum benefit from, explicit pedagogic strategies. Here one can see a homology – and perhaps more than a homology, Bourdieu acknowledges Bernstein's work[12] – with the seminal work of Basil Bernstein on linguistic codes and the classification and framing of knowledge. The distinctive pedagogic works of different groups or classes do not merely differ with respect to explicitness, but also inasmuch as they inculcate different dispositions to acquire the 'particular type of symbolic mastery that is privileged by the dominant cultural arbitrary'.[13] This is at the root of the critical educational distinction between the theoretical or the scientific and the practical or the technical, exemplified by the vocational distinction between the engineer and the technician.

There is, at this point, an intriguing and convincing further twist in the argument. In a social formation – such as most advanced industrial societies – where the dominant culture favours 'symbolic mastery' over 'practical mastery', the dominant pedagogic work, particularly in secondary education, will lean heavily on the *implicit* inculcation of that symbolic mastery. This will privilege the dominant groups or classes because they will already have acquired the basic dispositions of that symbolic mastery – talking and manipulating culture, rather than making things – and therefore its implicit inculcation is, for them, 'preaching to the converted'.

Thus in two ways the dominated are disadvantaged. With respect to formalised, 'scientific', elite knowledge, they are less able to take advantage of the explicit pedagogic strategies which are the medium of its inculcation. On the other hand, the less obvious symbolic mastery which constitutes the defining culture of the elite – the cultural distinction of the dominant – is rendered remote and mysterious because it is only ever implicitly communicated to them. By virtue of their upbringing they lack the necessary practical mastery which is required to recognise it without recognising it, hence they cannot acquire it competently or authentically.

Finally, Bourdieu moves on to a series of propositions which are specifically about those systems of symbolic violence (educational systems) which depend on institutionalised schools. One of the most important characteristics of institutionalised educational systems is their role in reproducing the conditions of their own existence. They have to reproduce themselves as distinct fields, differentiated from other fields. In the creation of an apparently autonomous educational system there is a reciprocal relationship of mutual reinforcement between structural processes of institutionalisation and the professional interests of those who monopolise pedagogic work (teachers). The latter becomes formalised into a homogeneous and orthodox 'work of schooling'. This routinised work produces a standardised and ritualised school culture within which these agents of the educational system reinforce their own value by ensuring the reproduction of the (educational) market which bestows that value upon them.

The pedagogic authority of the school is the source of the illusion that the symbolic violence exercised by the educational system is unrelated to the overall structure of power relations, inasmuch as it fosters a view of schooling as a legitimate or neutral process. One of the ways in which it does this is by facilitating the limited social mobility of a limited number of members of the dominated group or class. This illusion is further fostered in state educational systems by the fact that education is not paid for directly: it appears to have the open access of being 'free'. The work which teachers do therefore appears as 'disinterested' and motivated solely by ideals of education and learning. Thus is symbolic violence misrecognised and social structure reproduced in the process of cultural reproduction.

This summary may have done some disservice to the complexity of Bourdieu's theory of symbolic violence: it does, however, accurately present the bones of the argument. The first thing to note is that, although he appears to go to enormous lengths to avoid using the word,[14] what we are offered here is a general theory of *socialisation*. It is also other things, a theory of ideology being among them, but it is certainly about socialisation and, as such, can be seen to have affinities in some respects with structural functionalist accounts of the same process.[15] The second thing is that this is Bourdieu – despite the language

– at his most systematic and rigorous. It is difficult but it is relatively clear. Finally, it has most if not all of the problems which were discussed in Chapter Four: the habitus remains a 'black box', for example, the argument is essentially deterministic and institutions remain shadowy and inadequately constituted in theoretical terms. In the next section we will examine the development of this theoretical model in the context of empirical studies of the French education system.

CULTURAL REPRODUCTION AND SOCIAL REPRODUCTION

There are three main texts which I will draw upon to outline Bourdieu's substantive sociology of education. *The Inheritors*, a study of 'French students and their relation to culture' co-authored with Passeron[16] was first published in France in 1964. The empirical research it draws upon was undertaken in the early 1960s and the analysis bears the obvious mark of ideas deriving from Bourdieu's Algerian research. *Reproduction in Education, Society and Culture*, to which extensive reference has already been made, draws upon slightly later research and was published first in 1970. It remains the best known of all Bourdieu's works. Finally, one of his most readable works is a paper summarising the argument, entitled 'Cultural Reproduction and Social Reproduction', which first appeared in French in 1971, being published in English in 1973, since when it has been much anthologised.[17] A slightly earlier English version of part of that paper provides us with a concise summary of Bourdieu's sociology of education:

> the sociology of educational institutions and, in particular, of higher educational institutions, may make a decisive contribution to the frequently neglected aspect of the sociology of power which consists in the science of the dynamics of class relations. Indeed, among all the solutions provided, throughout the course of history, to the problem of the transmission of power and privileges, probably none have been better dissimulated and, consequently, better adapted to societies which tend to reject the most patent forms of hereditary transmission of power and privileges, than that provided by the educational system in contributing to the reproduction of the structure of class relations and in dissimulating the

fact that it fulfils this function under the appearance of neutrality.[18]

Bourdieu, in the 1960s, successfully sought to make a break with an over-specialised, ploddingly empirical and bureaucratised sociology of education, integrating the study of education into a wider field concerned with power, inequality and social order. The first major work in which he did so was *The Inheritors*.

Based on surveys and case-studies of Arts Faculty students in Lille and Paris, supported by national higher education statistics, *The Inheritors* is essentially a study of the production and reproduction of cultural privilege. Although it is a fragmentary text – three short reports on separate areas of research with a Conclusion tacked on at the end – much of the argument foreshadows *Reproduction* and the theory of symbolic violence. Choice of discipline and attitude to education, for example, are produced by family background. Those factors which make pupils/students 'at home' in an educational institution, which are the product of family education, create or reproduce class inequalities in achievement. The subtlety of the reproduction of privilege is one of the main themes. Bourdieu argues that the system consecrates privilege by ignoring it, by treating everybody as if they were equal when, in fact, the competitors all begin with different handicaps based on cultural endowment. Privilege becomes translated into 'merit'. For some, higher education is an effort and a constant struggle; for others, members of the dominant classes, it is their legitimate heritage. We also find familiar themes: the unconscious nature of the process at work, allied to a version of the 'subjective expectation of objective probabilities':

The weight of cultural heredity is such it is here possible to possess exclusively without even having to exclude others, since everything takes place as if the only people excluded were those who excluded themselves . . . These determinisms do not need to be consciously perceived in order to force subjects to take their decisions in terms of them, in other words, in terms of the *objective future* of their social category.[19]

Thus, the legitimatory authority of the school system can multiply social inequalities because the most disadvantaged classes, too conscious of their destiny and too unconscious of the ways in which it is brought about, thereby help to bring it upon themselves.[20]

Reproduction and the later article expand and develop these arguments. The dominant culture – the cultural arbitrary – is misrecognised as legitimate by subordinate classes. However, despite this legitimacy, members of these classes stand in a different relationship to it than do the dominant groups by virtue of the differences in class habitus of each. The habitus of each group is generated by their contrasting positions within the 'objective structures' of society, and the different subjective expectations of the objective probabilities attaching to their respective class locations:

> the disposition to make use of the School and the predispositions to succeed in it depend, as we have seen, on the objective chances of using it and succeeding in it that are attached to the different social classes, these dispositions and predispositions in turn constituting one of the most important factors in the perpetuation of the structure of educational chances as an objectively graspable manifestation of the relationship between the educational system and the system of class relations. Even the negative dispositions and predispositions leading to self-elimination, such as, for example, self-depreciation, devalorization of the School and its sanctions or resigned expectation of failure or exclusion may be understood as unconscious anticipation of the sanctions the School objectively has in store for the dominated classes.[21]

The pedagogic process is legitimated through mutually dependent ideologies of equality of opportunity and meritocratic achievement. Bourdieu's central theme in his analysis of education is that, since what is being inculcated is the dominant cultural arbitrary, excellence and scholastic achievement will naturally be defined in terms of that arbitrary cultural paradigm. It therefore follows that pupils whose familial socialisation bestows upon them the appropriate level of cultural capital – both more of it and of the 'right' kind – will necessarily achieve more academically than those whose relationship to the cultural arbitrary is more distant. The habitus of the subordinated class(es) will, in generating an acceptance of the system's legitimacy, reinforce their disadvantage by inhibiting their demands for access to the higher reaches of education by defining it as 'not for the likes of us'. At every rung on the educational ladder they will tend to eliminate themselves. The process of cultural reproduction reproduces the class relations of the social structure.

There is a twofold cultural reproduction of the legitimacy of domination: as a legitimate educational process based on notions of scholastic merit and as a system of legitimate class positions ('the likes of us'). Within such a system there is a close relationship between membership of the cultural and economic elites. However, Bourdieu goes on to argue that the less-than-perfect congruence between membership of the two elites further contributes to the legitimacy of their superordination. The fact that most members of the economic elite also belong to the cultural elite enables their dominance to be justified as resting upon superior intellectual abilities. On the other hand, the fact that some members of the cultural elite are not economically privileged, and vice versa – this is the argument about the functions of limited social mobility – is seen as proof positive of the inherent fairness of a meritocratic education system, through which *in theory* all can pass, irrespective of their economic capital.[22] Thus are the existing power relations of class society reproduced in their legitimate embodiment as the cultural arbitrary.

This analysis is open to exactly the same criticisms as the general theory of practice discussed in Chapter Four. Despite the stated project – the escape from 'reifying abstractions' by the generation of 'relational concepts',[23] the way in which Bourdieu uses concepts such as 'subjectivity' and 'objectivity' throughout implies a causal model predicated upon a materialist determination (admittedly 'in the last instance') and a consequent abstraction and reification of social structure. What is more, the difficulties attached to his notion of the 'subjective expectation of objective probabilities' are emphasised and given a new twist by Bourdieu's introduction of the concept of 'misrecognition'.

The attempt to fit these concepts together exposes three distinct problems. The manner in which they are combined can be summarised as follows. Actors' subjective knowledge and expectations apprehend the objective future attached to their social location, but only up to a point, only in a limited fashion. At that point misrecognition of their future as legitimate inhibits the formulation of alternative, 'objectively' more accurate propositions about the social world.

The relationship between these contrasting modes of knowledge is problematic and contradictory. The initial problem concerns the necessity to Bourdieu's theory that the proletariat should understand and perceive a present and, even more problematically, a future in which their domination is somehow objectively constituted, and the equally necessary systematic misperception of that present and future as legitimate by the same class. This is surely contradictory, if only inasmuch as the first entails an experience of domination as *inevitable* or 'natural' while the second implies that people *elect* to occupy their positions of social disadvantage.

Second, in order to attempt the mediation of subjective expectations and misrecognition within the same framework, Bourdieu is forced to posit that the former is an unconscious and the latter a conscious process. Of the two opposing modes of knowledge, only one – misrecognition as a result of ideology – is readily available to the sociologist via the speech acts or other communications of research subjects. How the other, the 'real' motive force of behaviour, is to be determined remains, at first glance, a mystery.[24]

This epistemological puzzle is solved, however, by a sleight of hand which creates a third problem. Bourdieu elides the necessary distinction between folk or common-sense models and knowledge, on the one hand, and analytical models and knowledge, on the other. This elision is latent rather than manifest most of the time – and it is also present, as we have already discussed, in his general theory of practice – but occasionally the veil parts and the legerdemain is revealed, as in the following:

> . . . the objective probability of entering this or that stage of education that is attached to a class is not just an expression of the unequal representation of the different classes in the stage of education being considered . . . rather *it is a theoretical construction providing one of the most powerful principles of explanation of these inequalities*.[25]

The 'objective probability' which the dominated classes 'subjectively perceive' – albeit via their (collective?) unconscious – thus turns out to be nothing more than the calculations of the sociologist. Casting himself in the role of *deus ex machina*, every move which Bourdieu makes underlines the determinism of his model.

Bourdieu's sociology of education became enormously popular in the late 1970s and early 1980s, generating a large critical literature.[26] In particular it seemed to offer the Left a means of inserting *agency* – Marxian praxis – into the pessimism and structural determinism of authors such as Althusser, without losing a theoretical grasp on the structured edifice of capitalist exploitation and class inequality. Insofar as this literature was critical – and it was often surprisingly uncritical[27] – it can be sorted into a number of strands which I shall exemplify here as (a) an empirical critique from mainstream sociology, and (b) a theoretical critique from the Left.

Empirically, this model of the reproduction of cultural capital within the family and at school came under fire from the Oxford Social Mobility Project. Basing their critique upon the Project's data concerning educational success – as indicated by formal examination results – and social class, the authors argue that Bourdieu's concept of cultural capital as a 'primordial' or initial handicap disregards the importance of the social mobility which is encouraged by a state education system:

> the state selective schools (much more than the private schools) were doing far more than 'reproducing' cultural capital; they were creating it too. They were bringing an academic or technical training to a very substantial number of boys from homes that were not in any formal sense educated.[28]

Halsey and his colleagues conclude that although cultural capital *is* important in influencing selection for secondary school, thereafter its importance is slight, social class being the most important source of differential achievement in secondary education.[29] The overall tenor of their analysis emphasises the *dissemination* of cultural capital, rather than its hierarchical *reproduction*.

It might be said at this point that their critique is misplaced: France, after all, is a very different place from England with regard to both class relations and institutionalised education. Bourdieu and Passeron are, however, explicit that their overall theoretical scheme, which they exemplify and explore using French data, is intended to have wide, general applicability. The Oxford critique is, however, deficient in at least two other important respects.

First, the concept of cultural capital which they employ is different from Bourdieu's. They use parental academic achievement as an indicator of the amount of cultural capital circulating in the home and formal examination achievement as an indicator of the inter-generational transmission of cultural capital. His is a much wider, less specific concept: language use, manners and orientations/dispositions. These are 'subtle modalities in the relationship to culture and language'.[30] Further, Bourdieu is clear that the full social value of educational qualifications is only realisable in the appropriate context. Hence, in themselves, they do not indicate very much:

> The same academic qualifications receive very variable values and functions according to the economic and social capital . . . which those who hold these qualifications have at their disposal and according to the markets in which they use them.[31]

In Halsey *et al.*'s defence, Bourdieu does at times – as in the final sentence of the article from which the quotation above is drawn[32] – imply an equivalence between cultural capital and formal qualifications. More recently – in *Homo Academicus*, a study of French higher education – Bourdieu does, in fact, use school attended and formal examination success as indicators of 'cultural capital, inherited or acquired'.[33] Nonetheless, his theory as tested by Halsey *et al.* differentiates sharply between cultural capital and formal educational credentials. Certainly the Oxford Project's measures of cultural capital are not an adequate basis for refuting his argument.

In the second place, given the importance which the Oxford team attach to secondary schooling as a causal factor inhibiting or promoting educational mobility,[34] it seems clear that if, as they themselves conclude, cultural capital (by their definition) is an important factor influencing selection for secondary education – either for school in a selective system or stream in comprehensive education – then it does play a vital role in generating the relationship between origins and destinations in capitalist society.

Allowing for these reservations, the major findings of the Oxford project indicate persuasively that the educational institutions of class society do not reproduce social inequality in the clear-cut fashion suggested by Bourdieu. While acknowledging the significance of limited social mobility in social reproduction, his model is too rigid and more deterministic than sophisticated analyses of the facts allow. As Goldthorpe has argued, Bourdieu's theoretical reach exceeds the supporting evidence of his data.[35] Recent research which demonstrates the difference which individual schools and their methods and organisation can make to the educational outcomes of their pupils further supports this line of argument against Bourdieu.[36] So does the long tradition of research which insists that there is, at best, only a modest positive correlation between formal educational achievement and economic/occupational outcomes.[37] From whatever direction, empirical research suggests that the link between education and class does not appear to be as tight as Bourdieu's model of social reproduction would have it.

Coming to the theoretical critique from the Left, two authors will serve as examples. Making points about Bourdieu's sociology of education which support, in some respects, the critique of the theory of practice set out in Chapter Four, Sharp[38] convicts Bourdieu on the following charges: (1) his theory of educational selection is basically a theory of cultural deprivation, akin to the controversial 'culture of poverty' model; (2) he inadequately analyses the institutional and social context of schooling; (3) his model of classes and power is inadequate, depending solely on a hierarchical occupational structure and social status; (4) his theory is ahistorical; and (5) he almost completely ignores the role of the state in social and cultural reproduction. All of these criticisms have considerable merit. She also accuses Bourdieu of being a Weberian rather than a Marxist. Since he has, however, always denied being either, this is hardly likely to keep him awake at night.

Connell, in one of the best critiques of social reproduction theories,[39] offers a slightly different set of criticisms which, once again, resonates with my general argument in Chapter Four. First, Bourdieu's model of classes and class relations is, at best, taken for granted and, at worst, untheorised: classes are 'just there'. Second, there is an absence of dynamics or process in the model, particularly at the level of the system. This leads to a form of functionalism. Third, and it is a related point, the theory is ahistorical. This leads to the next, and most damning criticism, that social reproduction is a chimera, it doesn't actually happen. To argue that it does is to ignore the 'intelligible succession' of history and the transformations of structure which characterise history. There may be ongoing similarities – no, there *will* be – but there is also change: today is produced (by people, who else?) out of yesterday. Next, he argues that the concept of the habitus is a 'black box', which remains a mystery in terms of process. What is more, Bourdieu's model of socialisation and individual development is over-cognitive, neglecting many dimensions of human psychology (the emotions, in particular). Finally, he suggests that the general theory of symbolic violence is too ambitious, failing to acknowledge 'the intrinsic and integral historicity of class processes'.[40] Such are the differences between cultures and epochs that one theory cannot hope to allow for them. These criticisms must also be acknowledged as telling.

The central thread which unites the empirical and theoretical critiques is the argument that Bourdieu's theory of cultural reproduction and social reproduction is deterministic. It fails to allow or account for social change at the level of the system and does not allow for meaningful agency or process at the individual level. It is ahistorical. In general, it is a self-perpetuating, mechanical model of society which sits ill with observed reality. Crucial aspects of society are inadequately theorised (institutions and groups/classes once again). To reiterate Connell's most important point, social reproduction as a model of how capitalist society manages to keep the working class quiescent is probably *wrong*:

> The care and maintenance of capitalist domination in the industrialised countries . . . is . . . best served by *preventing* the construction of the working class as a well-defined social entity, and, to the extent that it is politically and socially mobilised, by *sabotaging* its 'social reproduction'.[41]

Connell is here alluding to the real long-term transformations – the welfare state, broadened home ownership, increased affluence – which have characterised the post-war history of western, capitalist societies. These suggest an understanding of the maintenance of relative social stability that is rather different to Bourdieu's. Further, to return to one of Sharp's points, these are trends which are the result of political action by the *state*, precisely aimed, among other things, at the creation of a middle-range consensus which includes large sections of the working class(es). To reformulate Connell's point: to maintain order and secure capitalism what may be needed is the production of new class relations, rather than the reproduction of the old.

Connell does not wholly reject Bourdieu's theory, however.

He acknowledges the excitement of Bourdieu's writings: 'he is one of the very few systematic social theorists to have a way of talking about what living in the world is really like, its shadows and its sunlight, its langours and its teeth'.[42] The notion of cultural capital, what's more, isn't absurd; its problem is that it 'exaggerates a good insight'.[43] In general, Bourdieu's project – and that of the other reproduction theorists (such as Althusser) – remains of enormous importance: how does a social system in which a substantial section of the population are obviously disadvantaged and exploited survive without its rulers having to depend on physical coercion for the maintenance of order? It is an old question, the persistent asking of which may be of greater importance than the prospect of a definitive answer.

In his theory of symbolic violence, Bourdieu argues that one characteristic of institutionalised education systems is that they must assume responsibility for their own continued functioning and reproduction. This theme does not receive explicit attention in the second, research-based part of *Reproduction*. For that we must turn to *Homo Academicus*, published nearly fifteen years later.

FEAR AND LOATHING IN NANTERRE

Bourdieu's analysis of the French university system, which was first published in French in 1984,[44] is both specific and general. It is specific inasmuch as he makes few concessions to the reader with a less than complete familiarity with that system. It is a highly indexical account. Many of the observations which he makes, however, are likely to prove very familiar to the British or American academic reader. Herein lies its generality.

It is an analysis of a world with which Bourdieu is not only intimate but of which he is a member. In terms of method or approach it is, by comparison with the crunched numbers of *Reproduction*, a return to qualitative, quasi-ethnographic research. It is the anthropologist come home: an 'epistemological experiment', an exercise in 'participant objectivation'. And, indeed, it begins with a taxing essay about epistemology – the issues which we have already looked at in Chapter Three – and the role of writing style and language use in the 'objectification of objectification'. This specific part of Bourdieu's argument in *Homo Academicus* – about the nature and function of academic language – will be discussed in Chapter Seven.

As an insider's view of French universities, *Homo Academicus* has much to recommend it. By the discipline's defining criterion of exoticism it may not be *real* anthropology, but it may yet turn out to be Bourdieu's *best* anthropology. While it does address the issue of the reproduction of the institutions of higher education in France, it approaches the question from a standpoint which is different in important respects from the perspective suggested by the theory of symbolic violence. The difference is difficult to characterise, but in the intervening period it is as if the inexorable *logic* of reproduction has receded from view somewhat, replaced in part by a more open, less rigid analytical stance.

As with so much of Bourdieu's work, the basic argument is actually neither novel nor radical. Culture and the means of cultural (re)production – in this case, the elite institutions of higher education – are resources and weapons in the struggle over economic and political hierarchy and domination. They are also the terrain over which those struggles take place. Culture is thus both a means and an end, simultaneously. The influence of Weber here is clear: for *culture*, in Bourdieu's case, read *status*, in Weber's. The equivalence is only approximate – status probably encompasses both cultural and social capital – but it is revealing. Culture, and the institutions of cultural production, categorisation and registration (legitimation), are things *with* which people fight, *about* which they fight, and the ground *over* which they fight. Whether it be New Guinea, New York or *Le Nouvel Observateur*, the principle is the same (although the practice is different). Anthropologists 'discovered' this years ago, not to mention Nancy Mitford.[45]

Conflicts over culture and its legitimation take place within the academic field and within the broader 'field of external power'. Each field is organised according to two contrasting and antagonistic principles of hierarchy: the social hierarchy of inherited economic capital and political power, versus the cultural hierarchy of symbolic capital – in this context, academically consecrated knowledge – and intellectual *gravitas*. Each of these in turn relates to competing principles of legitimation: the temporal and political, on the one hand, and the scientific and intellectual, on the other. Within the universities the 'conflict of the faculties' (Bourdieu borrows an expression from Kant here) is the expression of a class hierarchy – in terms of the social origins of staff and students – which extends up from science, via the social sciences, arts and humanities, to the elites of law and medicine. Academic excellence varies in inverse proportion to position in the social hierarchy of the faculties, and is related to different models of academic practice and the significance of professional heredity in each field:

> The faculties which are dominant in the political order have the function of training executive agents able to put into practice without questioning or doubting . . . the techniques and recipes of a body of knowledge which they claim neither to produce nor to transform; on the contrary, the faculties which are dominant in the cultural order are destined to arrogate to themselves, in their need to establish a rational basis for the knowledge which the other faculties simply inculcate and apply, a freedom which is withheld from executive activities . . .[46]

Within each faculty the same hierarchy – social/political competence as opposed to scientific/intellectual competence – structures the institutional field.

Academic power, the ability to influence both the expectations which other people have and their 'objective probability' of fulfilling them, is related to the hierarchy of social capital and political competence. Intellectual and scientific criteria come a poor second, as is demonstrated by Bourdieu's exquisite dissection of the use of implicit criteria of acceptability (social competence, whether or not someone's 'face fits') in academic recruitment.[47] This argument is further advanced in his discussion of 'the categories of professorial judgement'.[48] Using sources such as student files, references and obituaries, he explores the subtleties of characterisation and description involved in making academic judgements about colleagues and students. An officially defined and specifically *academic* classificatory vocabulary allows the intrusion and ultimate importance of criteria of *social* classification (and, at the same time, masks their presence). 'Dull' or 'just about acceptable' are both, for example, ways of saying 'petty bourgeois' without ever having said it. Thus is the social composition of the academic field reproduced: like recruits like.

It is not, however – and this is a further refreshing departure from his earlier work – a static or unchanging picture. There is the new predomination of science and technology, threatening the *ancien régime* of doctors and lawyers with a loss of power (if not of prestige). Social science has become doubly subordinate. The academic world, if not turned upside down, has become more complex.

The shadow of May 1968, the zenith of French student radical-ism and the broad period to which much of Bourdieu's data belongs, is also cast long over the analysis. Caught between an increase in student numbers and a consequent devaluation of diplomas, the 'new' disciplines (such as sociology) were at the intersection of two 'latent crises of maximum intensity'.[49] The first stemmed from the gap between student expectations and likely outcomes. Here, for the first time, Bourdieu looks in depth at a situation where 'subjective expectations' and 'objective probabilities' are out of kilter with each other. On the one hand there were upper-class students low on formal academic attainment; on the other, middle-class students short on social capital. Neither, albeit for different reasons, were likely to end up where they hoped they *might* or expected they *should*. The second crisis arose within the cohort of teachers drawn into the universities by the *arriviste* disciplines. With expectations raised by their admission to the collegial ranks of the universities, they were held down in the lower ranks of the institutional hierarchy because of their lack of social capital. Thus, out of a series of unfavourable cultural and social exchange rates operating within the market of the academic field, were born the 'events' of May 1968 and student revolt, if not revolution.

The point is, of course, that it was, at most, only a revolt. The break in the circle linking 'expectation and opportunities' was an 'objective break' (changed circumstances again), which the individuals affected had no hand in producing.[50] As such, it may have permitted them to step outside the circle – which is actually a trap – and reject the rules of the game which govern the competition for position within the academic field in favour of a revolutionary questioning of the nature of the game itself. Since this is not what happened, we are forced to speculate that either subjective expectations were readjusted in the light of unchanging objective probabilities, or the probabilities them-selves changed. Bourdieu, unfortunately, does not tell us which.

There are other problems, all of which will be familiar by now. There is, for example, a lack of historical and political context. Despite his protestations about the need to situate the universit-ies within the wider fields of social, economic and political power – thereby demythologising their claims to disinterested scholar-ship (and one may question whether these claims actually *needed* demythologising) – the analysis remains inward-looking and framed within an elitist self-regard. This allows the events of May 1968 to be discussed and explained without serious reference to the role of organised labour or parallel social movements elsewhere in Europe.

This highlights the more serious flaw in the analysis: a lack of clarity in Bourdieu's understanding of the nature and sources of power, an inability to understand resistance which derives from the basic determinism of his sociology.[51] Power is treated almost as a natural force – fields are, remember, 'fields of forces' – which flows through the system from top to bottom, and against which there is only the possibility of a symbolic resistance which is doomed to eventual failure. Power may, in some senses, be arbitrary but it is not *just* arbitrary and it is not monolithic. Where does the power in the 'field of external power' come from? Here it is the shade not of Weber but of Nietzsche which lurks at Bourdieu's elbow.

Finally, here, in an analysis of a specific and relatively small-scale 'empirical' field, we have a chance to see what the concept of field is in practice and, in particular, how Bourdieu analyses institutions. In reality, a field appears very much as Bourdieu describes it in the abstract: it has empirical contents – institutions and agents – and empirical, institutionally defined boundaries. It is, in fact, institutionally *constituted*, which is something that Bourdieu is not explicit about. This actually makes the problem about the nature and status of fields more rather than less difficult. Bourdieu, as I have already suggested, has no sociological model of institutions and how they work: this is another 'black box'. What he seems to mean when he talks about institutions, or, rather, how he constitutes them sociologically, is as a category of data about the individuals who work in them, or are otherwise 'members'. Bourdieu needs to take seriously the question of how the actions or practices of institutions differ from those of individuals (and how each becomes translated into the other; this is after all at the heart of why institutions exist). Despite the availability of a large literature, deriving once again from Weber, about how institutions are run and controlled, bureaucracy as a specifically modern social form, formality and informality, inter- and intra-organisational politics, etc., there is an absence here which is truly striking. And it *does* matter, given the centrality of the linked topics of power and domination in Bourdieu's thinking. Power and domination are among the most important concerns and characteristics of organisations and institutions. They demand better treatment than Bourdieu gives them.

Homo Academicus is not just about higher education. It is also about culture and status, culture as an object and means of struggle, culture as a marker of social identity. This is a long-standing theme in Bourdieu's work, extending all the way back to his Algerian days. It is to this topic, the competition for cultural distinction, that we will turn in the next chapter.

NOTES AND REFERENCES

[1] M. Weber, *Economy and Society*, ed. G. Roth and C. Wittich, Berkeley, University of California Press (1978), pp. 212–301, 941–55.

[2] P. Bourdieu and J.-C. Passeron, *Reproduction in Education, Society and Culture*, London, Sage (1977).

[3] R.W. Connell, *Which Way Is Up?*, Sydney, George Allen and Unwin Australia (1983), p. 145. This is a slightly modified quotation, in order to allow its use in my own sentence.

[4] P. Bourdieu and J.-C. Passeron, *Reproduction*, *op. cit.*, p. 5.

[5] *Ibid.*, p. xiii

[6] *Ibid.*, p. xi.

[7] *Ibid.*, p. 10.

[8] *Ibid.*, p. 31.

[9] *Ibid.*, p. 39.

[10] *Ibid.*, p. 47.

[11] *Ibid.*, p. 49.

[12] *Ibid.*, p. 133. For a discussion of the relationship between Bernstein's sociology of education and Bourdieu's, see: P. Atkinson, *Language, Structure and Reproduction*, London, Methuen (1985).

[13] P. Bourdieu and J.-C. Passeron, *Reproduction*, *op. cit.*, p. 50.

[14] R. Nice, personal communication.

[15] T. Parsons, *The Social System*, London, Routledge and Kegan Paul (1951), pp. 201–26. Where Bourdieu's account is particularly deficient by comparison with Parsons is in his lack of interest in the social construction of personality and motivation (see pp. 226–35 of *The Social System*). In making

this point I am echoing a comment made by R.W. Connell, *Which Way Is Up?*, *op. cit.*, p. 152.

[16] P. Bourdieu and J.-C. Passeron, *The Inheritors: French Students and Their Relation to Culture*, Chicago, University of Chicago Press (1979).

[17] P. Bourdieu, 'Cultural Reproduction and Social Reproduction', in R. Brown (ed.), *Knowledge, Education and Cultural Change*, London, Tavistock (1973).

[18] Centre for European Sociology, *Current Research*, Paris, École Pratique des Hautes Etudes (1972), pp. 11–12.

[19] P. Bourdieu and J.-C. Passeron, *The Inheritors*, *op. cit.*, p. 27.

[20] *Ibid.*, p. 72.

[21] P. Bourdieu and J.-C. Passeron, *Reproduction*, *op. cit.*, pp. 204–5.

[22] P. Bourdieu, 'Cultural Reproduction and Social Reproduction', *op. cit.*, pp. 97–9.

[23] P. Bourdieu and J.-C. Passeron, *Reproduction*, *op. cit.*, p. 102.

[24] *Ibid.*, pp. 78, 226, for clear examples of the problem.

[25] *Ibid.*, p. 156, my emphasis.

[26] In addition to Connell's essay, cited above, see *inter alia* the following: H. Giroux, 'Power and Resistance in the New Sociology of Education: Beyond Theories of Social and Cultural Reproduction', *Curriculum Perspectives*, vol. 2 (1982) no. 3, pp. 1–13; R.K. Harker, 'On Reproduction, Habitus and Education', *British Journal of Sociology of Education*, vol. 5 (1984), pp. 118–27; D. Swartz, 'Pierre Bourdieu: The Cultural Transmission of Social Inequality', *Harvard Educational Review*, vol. 47 (1977), pp. 545–55; P. Willis, 'Cultural Production and Theories of Reproduction', in L. Barton and S. Walker (eds), *Race, Class and Education*, London, Croom Helm (1983).

[27] This lack of critical edge continues to characterise much of the commentary on Bourdieu's work; it afflicts both R. Harker, C. Maher and C. Wilkes (eds), *An Introduction to the Work of Pierre Bourdieu*, London, Macmillan (1990), and D. Robbins *The Work of Pierre Bourdieu*, Buckingham, Open University Press (1991).

[28] A.H. Halsey, A.F. Heath and J.M. Ridge, *Origins and Destinations: Family, Class and Education in Modern Britain*, Oxford, Clarendon Press (1980), p. 77.

[29] *Ibid.*, p. 200.
[30] P. Bourdieu, 'Cultural Reproduction and Social Reproduction', *op. cit.*, p. 82.
[31] *Ibid.*, p. 97.
[32] *Ibid.*, p. 99.
[33] P. Bourdieu, *Homo Academicus*, Cambridge, Polity (1988), pp. 230–2.
[34] A.H. Halsey *et al.*, *Origins and Destinations*, *op. cit.*, pp. 148–73.
[35] J.H. Goldthorpe, with C. Llewellyn and C. Payne, *Social Mobility and Class Structure in Modern Britain*, Oxford, Clarendon Press (1980), p. 58.
[36] P. Mortimore, P. Sammons, L. Stoll, D. Lewis and R. Ecob, *School Matters*, Berkeley, University of California Press (1988); M. Rutter, B. Maughan, P. Mortimore and J. Owston, *Fifteen Thousand Hours*, London, Open Books (1979); D. Reynolds, M. Sullivan and S. Murgatroyd, *The Comprehensive Experiment*, London, Falmer (1987); D.J. Smith and S. Tomlinson, *The School Effect*, London, Policy Studies Institute (1989).
[37] R. Boudon, *Education, Opportunity and Social Inequality*, New York, Wiley (1974); C. Jencks, M. Smith, H. Acland, M.J. Baine, D. Cohen, H. Gintis, B. Heyns and S. Michelson, *Inequality*, New York, Basic Books (1972); J. Oxenham (ed.), *Education Versus Qualifications?*, London, George Allen and Unwin (1984). For a counter argument, see: S. Bowles and H. Gintis, *Schooling in Capitalist America*, London, Routledge and Kegan Paul (1976).
[38] R. Sharp, *Knowledge, Ideology and the Politics of Schooling*, London, Routledge and Kegan Paul (1980), pp. 66–76.
[39] R.W. Connell, *Which Way Is Up?*, *op. cit.*, pp. 140–61.
[40] *Ibid.*, p. 119.
[41] *Ibid.*, p. 155.
[42] *Ibid.*, p. 153.
[43] R.W. Connell, D.J. Achendon, S. Kessler and G.W. Dowsett, *Making the Difference: Schools, Families and Social Divisions*, Sydney, George Allen and Unwin Australia (1982), p. 188.
[44] P. Bourdieu, *Homo Academicus*, Paris, Éditions de Minuit (1984).
[45] N. Mitford (ed.), *Noblesse Oblige*, London, Hamish Hamilton (1956).

[46] P. Bourdieu, *Homo Academicus*, *op. cit.*, p. 63.
[47] *Ibid.*, pp. 136–47.
[48] *Ibid.*, pp. 194–225.
[49] *Ibid.*, p. 170.
[50] *Ibid.*, p. 172.
[51] A similar point about *Homo Academicus* is made by F. Inglis, 'The conflict of the faculties', *Times Higher Education Supplement*, 30 September 1988, pp. 18–19.

6

Culture, Status and Distinction

People compete about culture and they compete with it. The very definition of what can legitimately be called culture – with a capital 'C' – is one of the sharpest bones of contention: is a pile of bricks Art, or is it a pile of bricks? Answer: it's Art when it's in an art gallery (or is it?). Here it is the boundaries of the field – the authority to define them *and* their substantive content – which are at stake.

Bourdieu has consistently attempted to offer a 'scientific' alternative to a Kantian aesthetic philosophy in which the purity of aesthetic contemplation derives from moral agnosticism and a disinterested or aloof perspective. According to Bourdieu this is neither 'pure' nor 'disinterested'. It is in fact a disposition which comes from affluence. It is 'the paradoxical product of conditioning by negative economic necessities – a life of ease – that tends to induce an active distance from necessity'.[1] It is the same affordable vagueness about the need to make a living which produces a cavalier attitude towards education on the part of upper-class students (who can afford to do badly at law, or brilliantly at a non-vocational subject such as philosophy; they can even afford to do badly at philosophy, although that might just look like vulgar conspicuous consumption). The model of pure aesthetic judgement which Kant philosophised in his *Critique of Judgement* is a key element of the dominant cultural arbitrary of western societies. Modernism may have generated conflict about *who* defines *what* as Culture or Art, but the basic presumption – that there is something to be defined – remains. This conflict may, in fact, have hardened the boundaries of taste: we live in a world of supposed postmodern eclecticism, but never have more 'experts' spent more time telling us what to think about matters Cultural.

Bourdieu's initial subversive tactic is the dissolution of Culture into culture (in the wide anthropological sense). And here we witness at work, once again, the 'objectification of objectification'. In the first move, a domain of practices and objects which are subjectively defined as Culture (or not) by the actors concerned is empirically constituted as an object for sociological analysis. In the second, the principles of definition which are at work in that first process of objectification are themselves objectified as something to be explained: the classificatory boundary between Culture and culture becomes revealed as arbitrary and one more manifestation of the reality of class relations.

The other consistent theme which emerges in this area of Bourdieu's work is his interest in struggles and competition over status: in Kabylia this is the 'sense of honour', in the French academic world or the salons of the *haute bourgeoisie*, it is 'cultural distinction':

> in my earliest analyses of honour . . . you find all the problems that I am still tackling today: the idea that struggles for recognition are a fundamental dimension of social life and that what is at stake in them is an accumulation of a particular form of capital, honour in the sense of reputation and prestige, and that there is, therefore, a specific logic behind the accumulation of symbolic capital . . .[2]

So Bourdieu is not just interested in cultural taste(s), but also in the way in which those tastes arise out of, and are mobilised in, struggles for social recognition or status. In the conjunction of status and cultural classification, Weber meets Durkheim in Bourdieu's work. Bryan Turner has summarised Bourdieu's interests nicely:

> social status involves practices which emphasize and exhi-
> bit cultural distinctions and differences which are a cru-
> cial feature of all social stratification . . . Status may be
> conceptualised therefore as lifestyle; that is, as the total-
> ity of cultural practices such as dress, speech, outlook
> and bodily dispositions . . . While status is about political
> entitlement and legal location within civil society, status
> also involves, and to a certain extent is, style.[3]

Bourdieu's sociology of culture is, therefore, a sociology of cultural consumption, the uses to which culture is put, and the
manner in which cultural categories are defined and defended.
You will look in vain in Bourdieu for a sociology of practices of
cultural *production* (one of the limited exceptions being his study
of photography,[4] but even here his attention is upon production
in a superficial sense: choice of subject, the appropriateness of
occasions, stereotypical rules of composition, etc.). This may
appear strange given his emphasis upon practice, improvisation,
the generative capacities of the habitus and the embodiment of
culture. These are all, one might say, obvious contributors to a
new and exciting understanding of the work, for example, of the
artist. If a puzzle it be, the reasons for this absence may lie in
some of the failings of his theory of practice: its weak grasp on
subjectivity, the processual and ontological mysteries of the habitus, its hostility to the notion of self-conscious deliberation and
calculation (and creation, after all, involves more than the inter-
vention of the muse of inspiration). If Bourdieu has yet to
develop a sociology of cultural production – whether of the most
humble or the most elevated kind – it may be simply because
he can't, not without a complete change of spots.

PHOTOGRAPHERS AND ART GALLERIES

Two books from the mid-1960s illustrate the longevity of Bourdieu's interest in the Cultural field. Neither is very substantial –
one is forced to question whether either would have seen the
light of day in English translation were it not for Bourdieu's
status as a currently rising intellectual stock – but they do offer
an insight into the development of his thought in this area as
well as providing the link between his Algerian ethnography
and *Distinction*. Both deal with cultural forms – museums and

photography – which, being cheap or cost-free in economic terms, are in theory equally open to all groups and classes.

The first, about photography, is a collection of essays by Bourdieu and others. It opens with a brief discussion of Bourdieu's anthropological framework and an argument that, because it is accessible to everyone in terms of technique and cost:

> photography as a practice or as a cultural work appears as a privileged means of apprehending, in their most authentic expression, the aesthetics (and ethics) of different groups or classes and particularly the popular 'aesthetic' which can, exceptionally, be manifested in it.[5]

Three groups of camera users were studied: villagers in the Béarn, Renault factory workers and members of photographic clubs in Lille. The study concluded that class determinisms – via the mediation of 'group symbolism' and individual practices – construct what is photographable, what are acceptable subjects. These are defined, in part, by notions about rules of *composition* and by understandings of which *occasions* can and should be dignified by photography. Photography is particularly associated with family life and its integration. In rural communities, the defining function of the camera is to solemnise and record 'those climactic moments of social life in which the group solemnly reaffirms its unity':[6] weddings, christenings, First Communion or whatever (although not funerals). Family holidays, which combine this function with the strange or the exotic, are recognised photographic occasions. Clerical workers, however, while they may use photography in similar ways to peasants:

> no longer enjoy the same simple, direct and perhaps comfortable relationship to it. Reference to the fine arts, imposed or recalled by the survey situation, always insinuates itself into their judgements on photography, most frequently ending up by disturbing their self-assurance.[7]

Photography thus serves to reveal the equivocal relationship between this group – white-collar workers – and 'scholarly culture'. They know it is there but are unsure of what their attitude towards it is or ought to be. More generally, the cultural status of photography is ambiguous. If it is an art it is only a minor one, hence 'barbarism and incompetence are of no more consequence than virtuosity'.[8] This ambiguity turns the 'privileged classes' away from photography. However, at the same time it permits its appropriation by artistic middle-class 'deviants' as 'a substitute within their reach for the consecrated practices [of Art] which remain inaccessible to them'.[9]

Bourdieu also develops a model, which will become familiar to us as this chapter progresses, of a 'hierarchy of legitimacies' with respect to cultural goods and tastes.[10] At the top there is the 'sphere of legitimacy', occupied by music, painting, sculpture, literature and the theatre, where consumers' judgements are defined by legitimate authorities: museums, universities, etc. At the bottom, in the 'sphere of the arbitrary', individual taste is the self-conscious arbiter of choice with respect to fashion, food, furniture, etc. In between, the 'sphere of the legitimisable' is occupied by jazz, the cinema and photography: 'One therefore passes from the fully consecrated arts . . . to signifying systems which are abandoned – at least at first glance – to the arbitrariness of individual taste . . .'[11] This is a crude model. In particular, it conceals what Bourdieu would himself have doubtless wished to reveal in a more detailed discussion, namely that each of these spheres is internally hierarchicised in terms of vulgarity or barbarism of taste. There is, for example, a world of difference between *haute cuisine* and a peasant *cassoulet*. What is more, the further we move away from cultural legitimacy, towards the arbitrariness of *individual* taste, the sharper is likely to be the *social* competition over definitions of vulgarity and barbarism. It is here that issues of status will be most pronounced.

The Love of Art, co-written with Alain Darbel and Dominique Schnapper, first appeared in 1969.[12] Between 1964 and 1965 a series of surveys were carried out of the visiting public of various art galleries and museums in France and elsewhere. The intention was to relate the social characteristics of the visitors to the nature and characteristics of the museums, on the one hand, and their orientations towards art and museums (as revealed in questions about attitudes and visiting practices), on the other.

The results are much as one might expect: 'so much trouble . . . to express a few obvious truths'.[13] However, these truths are not obvious to the 'art lover'. The critique of Kantian aesthetics is explicit, part and parcel of Bourdieu's critique of the dominant culture's aesthetic articles of faith:

> To perceive a work in a specifically aesthetic way, that is, as a signifier meaning nothing other than itself, con-

sists not, as is sometimes suggested, of regarding it 'without relating it to anything other than itself, either emotionally or intellectually', in other words surrendering oneself to the work taken in its irreducible uniqueness, but in picking out its *distinctive stylistic characteristics* by relating it to the works constituting the class of which it is a part, and to these works alone.[14]

In other words, art appreciation – aesthetics, in this context – is something that one *learns*. And the place where this learning takes place is usually school (but only, of course, certain kinds of schools and certain kinds of pupils). Admiration for art is not an innate predisposition; it is an arbitrary, i.e. cultural, product of a specific process of inculcation characteristic of the educational system as it applies to upper- and (some) middle-class families. These are 'cultivated families', with a family ethos of their own which constitutes the basis upon which formal education does its pedagogic work. However:

Inasmuch as it produces a culture which is simply the interiorization of the cultural arbitrary, family or school upbringing, through the inculcation of the arbitrary, results in an increasingly complete masking of the arbitrary nature of the inculcation. The myth of an innate taste . . . is just one of the expressions of the recurrent illusion of a cultivated nature predating any education, an illusion which is a necessary part of education as the imposition of an arbitrary . . .[15]

Cultivated individuals thus confront their own distinction as taken for granted and natural, a marker of their social value, their status. Bourdieu here makes the incisive comment that 'culture is only achieved by denying itself as such, namely as artificial and artificially acquired'.[16] Hence the real 'masters of the judgement of taste' can appear to rise above the dictates of culture, although they operate within them all the time.

The corollary of this is that the only people who exclude the working classes and the peasants from an enjoyment – or, rather, a *proper* enjoyment – of Art are themselves. For all concerned, it is not in their 'natures':

. . . the privileged classes of bourgeois society replace the difference between two cultures, products of history reproduced by education, with the basic difference

> between two natures, one nature naturally cultivated,
> and another nature naturally natural . . .Thus the sancti-
> fication of culture and art . . . fulfils a vital function by
> contributing to the consecration of the social order.[17]

Culture and Art meet social reproduction in a model of the social
construction of taste which, although it has a certain amount of
obvious authenticity, is somewhat too closed and neat to be
plausible. We will return to this theme when we discuss *Distinction* later in this chapter.

INTELLECTUAL FIELD AND CREATIVE PROJECT

The absence of a sociology of cultural production in Bourdieu's
work has already been noted. This may not, however, have been
wholly fair to Bourdieu's *intentions*, inasmuch as, in another of
his writings from the mid-1960s, he does attempt to assign to
'the sociology of intellectual and artistic creation' 'its proper
object and at the same time its limits':

> the relationship between a creative artist and his work,
> and therefore his work itself, is affected by the system
> of social relations within which creation as an act of
> communication takes place, or to be more precise, by
> the position of the creative artist in the structure of the
> intellectual field . . .[18]

This is clearly part of the same train of thought as Bourdieu's
analysis of photographic practices.[19] It is, however, somewhat
more ambitious, and of wider significance for the sociology of
culture.

First of all, Bourdieu identifies the *intellectual field*, within
which creation occurs. It is a system of agents or 'systems of
agents' – i.e. institutions – who in their relationships with each
other may be conceptualised as forces of differing strengths
which, in opposition or combination, structure the field at any
specific moment. These forces are defined by their position within
the field rather than by any intrinsic characteristics. They are
also defined by their participation in the *cultural field*, which he
defines as 'a system of relations between themes and problems'.[20]

Through the mediaeval and early modern periods, intellectual
and creative life was dominated, through mechanisms of patron-

age and censorship, by the Church and the Court functioning as external legitimising authorities. The dawning of modernity saw the gradual liberation of artists from these constraints and the eventual organisation of an autonomous intellectual field, characterised by 'specific authorities of selection and consecration' that were internal to the field and in competition with each other for cultural legitimacy. This historical process was a shift from the domination of the field by a small number of very powerful legitimising forces or agents, to something more like (or, indeed, actually) a market situation, in which a large number of individually less significant agents – publishers, theatre managers, critics, financiers, collectors – vie with others in the social construction of legitimate taste. It is this historical development of a 'relatively autonomous intellectual field' which allows the appearance of the 'independent intellectual, who does not recognise nor wish to recognise any obligations other than the intrinsic demands of his creative project'.[21]

What is this 'creative project'? It is: 'the place of meeting and sometimes of conflict between the *intrinsic necessity of the work of art* which demands that it be continued, improved and completed, and *social pressures* which direct the work from outside.'[22]

Bourdieu, quoting Paul Valéry, exemplifies the above distinction as a contact between works that are created by their public and works that create their own public. But he doesn't actually get us much closer to cultural creativity and production. In order for things to be 'continued, improved and completed' they must first be *begun*. And how that happens remains obscure. What Bourdieu is offering – and a similar point could be made about his wider body of work – is a sociology of art as the history of an immaculate conception's progress. Whatever art's 'intrinsic necessity' is, we are not told.

One important influence upon the classification of creative projects as legitimate endeavours is the 'objectivization achieved by criticism'.[23] The work becomes the object of others' valuations. It is in this way that the 'public meaning' of the work and its creator – and Bourdieu here is suggesting something stronger than reputation – comes to be established. This is a collective judgement on the 'value and truth of the work', in relation to which the author (or artist, or whatever) must define him or herself.[24] The autonomous intellectual is, of course, not autonomous at all. Creative projects are, in a sense, always collective projects, and matters of taste and aesthetic judgement, even the most individual or personal, contain within them a necessary reference to 'a common meaning already established'.

Which is where what Bourdieu calls the 'cultural unconscious' comes in: 'attitudes, aptitudes, knowledge, themes and problems, in short the whole system of categories of perception and thought acquired by the systematic apprenticeship which the school organizes or makes it possible to organize'.[25] In other words, the habitus as it is produced by the pedagogic work of the education system. This expresses itself in a range of effects: from 'unconscious borrowings and imitations' to the inspiration which derives from 'the common source of themes and forms which define the cultural tradition of a society and an age'.[26] But it is done unknowingly, and this masks the importance of society and culture, allowing the celebration – the misrecognition – of individual, autonomous creativity and the glorification of Culture. In the same way, the school can only do its work by denying the determinisms of social origins and culture and valorising ability and Education. In this, both – Culture and Education – are also legitimising the existing social relations of domination.

The canons of legitimacy – shared understandings of the nature of Art and Culture and of how they are classified – divide the cultural field and its vassal, the intellectual field, into the familiar three zones: universal legitimacy, contested legitimacy (where genres are in the process of legitimisation, or not) and the non-legitimacy of arbitrary personal taste. As we have already seen, these classificatory categories organise cultural consumption. Bourdieu is insisting that cultural production is thus classified also. These criteria of legitimacy are the constraints within which creativity works.

What he does *not* do is account for cultural production – and indeed consumption – which successfully challenges the boundaries or contents of these categories. How is the imperialism of legitimate Art broken or undermined? In Bourdieu's scheme of things it is difficult to understand the relatively modest innovation of Seurat, let alone the subsequent pace and profundity of change represented, say, by Cézanne or Picasso. To shift fields altogether, Stravinsky's *Rite of Spring* revolutionised the music of the concert hall; Elvis Presley's Sun sessions or Dylan's first electric performances did the same for popular music. But where do such impulses come from and how do they happen? There is something profoundly social going on here – explained by neither the critical marketplace nor the 'intrinsic' power of individual 'genius' (although in all of my examples there is that, whatever 'that' is, too) – but Bourdieu never quite gets round to broaching the topic. There is rebellion in his model but, alas, no revolution.

DISTINCTION

When *La Distinction* was first published in France in 1979, not only did it sell in surprisingly large numbers for a densely written, technically intimidating and lengthy sociological study, but it also became the focus of a lively public debate. The clue to understanding this unusual celebrity may be found in the fact that the people who bought and argued over the book were largely those about whom it was written, French bourgeois intellectuals for whom cultural distinction is not a trivial matter:

> French readers either rejected its findings in horror at the thought that they might be revealed as something other than the individualists they take pride in considering themselves to be, or embraced it as a major contribution to understanding modern society.[27]

Something more than individualism was at stake, however. This is Bourdieu's major assault on the notion of pure or innate cultural taste, and the whipping boy is, once again, Kant (not for nothing is the sub-title *A Social Critique of the Judgement of Taste*). Bourdieu's project is the 'barbarous reintegration of aesthetic consumption into the world of ordinary consumption (against which it endlessly defines itself)'[28]: Culture is dissolved into culture. Now at this point, some of you may be asking whether our hero is not, in fact, tilting at windmills; do people really believe, these days, in an ahistorical aesthetic sense which is independent of its social context? Well, sociologists and anthropologists may not, but some art historians and critics – and many more of their readers (not to mention those who do not read, but know what is art and what isn't) – certainly *do*. Here, for example, is Norman Bryson speaking: 'Painting and viewing are ultimately self-regulating activities . . . this is a *serene* system'.[29] Bourdieu's target here, is not quite a straw man. He has in his sights the consistent use of notions of 'taste' – as a sort of naturally occurring phenomenon – to mark and maintain (in part by masking the marking) social boundaries, whether these be between the dominant and dominated classes or within classes. Cultural classification systems, Bourdieu argues, are rooted in the class system.

The other task which Bourdieu sets himself in *Distinction* is the reconceptualisation of Weber's model of social stratification, in particular the relationship between class and *Stand* (status group). The concepts which he adopts to mediate between these are the class fraction and the life-style. Drawing upon two major surveys, undertaken in 1963 and 1967–8, of 1217 subjects from Paris, Lille and a small provincial town, supplemented by a wide range of data from other surveys concerned with a range of topics, the empirical meat of the book is concerned with the detailed explication of the life-style differences of differing class fractions.

It is a difficult and complex work to summarise. Presentationally, it is an intriguing pastiche of different blocks of text, photographs and diagrams, in the best traditions of *Actes de la recherche en sciences sociales*. Linguistically, it is at least as dense and unforgiving of a moment's lapse in concentration as any of its predecessors. As with his other studies of aspects of French society, Bourdieu is explicit that this is not *just* a study of France. The model he presents is 'valid beyond the particular French case and, no doubt, for every stratified society'.[30]

He begins on familiar ground: the link between cultural practices and social origins, mediated in large part through formal education. People *learn* to consume culture and this education is differentiated by social class. The further away one moves from the authorised hierarchy of preferences which is governed by legitimate Culture, the more one is concerned with 'non-legitimate' cultural domains, the greater becomes – in the absence of the legislation of orthodoxy – the influence of social origins upon practices and preferences.

At this point, Bourdieu presents us with a 'three-zone' model of cultural tastes: 'legitimate' taste, 'middle-brow' taste and 'popular taste'. Although at first sight this also is familiar, it is a little different to the model presented previously. That was a map of cultural *products* according to their legitimacy. This is a map of *tastes and preferences* which correspond to education level and social class; in short, it is the beginnings of a model of class *life-styles*.

Within this model of life-styles and cultural taste, the working-class aesthetic is a dominated aesthetic, constantly obliged to define itself by reference to the dominant aesthetic (the cultural arbitrary). In fact, the working class is, according to Bourdieu, less able than the middle or upper classes to adopt a specifically aesthetic point of view upon objects whose constitution and definition involves an aesthetic judgement; such an object might be anything from a car to a compact disc player to a photograph. The upper classes, distanced from necessity, are allowed a 'playful seriousness';[31] this aesthetic sense is part of an assured relation to the world, a sense of distinction:

> Like every sort of taste, it unites and separates. Being the product of the conditioning associated with a particular class of conditions of existence, it unites all those who are the product of similar conditions while distinguishing them from all others. And it distinguishes in an essential way, since taste is the basis of all that one has – people and things – and all that one is for others, whereby one classifies oneself and is classified by others.[32]

Apart from reminding us of the general social theory which underlies his analysis, this nicely gets to the heart of the matter: taste is one of the key signifiers and elements of social identity. It is one of the primary interactional determinants of class endogamy: individuals tend to meet and marry, or so Bourdieu argues, *within* rather than *between* life-styles (and, hence, within rather than between social classes).

The petite bourgeoisie fall, as one might imagine, rather badly between two stools. Condemned to differentiate themselves sharply from those immediately below them in the class system, they have essentially two problems concerning those above them. First, they may lack the education which is the basis for the mobilisation of legitimate taste. Second, and perhaps more important, they lack 'ease or cultivated naturalness', the familial habitus which enables the upper classes to disguise what they have *learned* as what they are *born* with. So even with appropriate schooling, the primary school teacher or the clerk is unlikely to be able to 'bring it off': another case of 'manners maketh the man'.

The structure of class life-styles is not, at first sight, obvious; its unity is 'hidden under the diversity and multiplicity of the set of practices performed in fields governed by different logics and therefore inducing different forms of realization'.[33] First, one must constitute the 'objective class' of people whose similar conditions of existence produce similar habituses and similar access to goods and power. This Bourdieu does by reference to occupation as an indicator of social class. Having done this, producing occupationally defined class fractions, he then examines national survey statistics for the economic capital (using indicators such as home ownership, luxury car ownership, income, etc.) and cultural capital (newspaper read, frequency of theatre-going, enthusiasm for classical music, etc.) possessed by the dominant class. The two forms of capital are inversely related: the more of one, the less of the other, a general rule which also holds good in the middle classes. This produces a rather more complex model of 'the space of social positions' – as structured by the differential distribution of *two* kinds of capital – than is commonly allowed for in simple up-down hierarchical models of stratification.[34] This is the interaction, in Weberian terms, of class and status.

Within this social space there are more kinds of mobility possible than simply upwards and downwards. In particular, transverse mobility is, suggests Bourdieu, of great importance. This is the result of conversion and reconversion strategies, when economic capital is 'cashed in' to obtain cultural capital in the next generation, and vice versa (although the former is probably more common than the latter). These strategies can accelerate the competition over access to elite education, for example, leading to 'diploma inflation'. It is central to Bourdieu's argument at this point that:

> Reproduction strategies, the set of outwardly very different practices whereby individuals or families tend, unconsciously and consciously, to maintain or increase their assets and consequently to maintain or improve their position in the class structure, constitute a system which, being the product of a single unifying, generative principle, tends to function and change in a systematic way. Through the mediation of the disposition towards the future, which is itself determined by the group's objective chances of reproduction, these strategies depend, first, on the volume and composition of the capital to be reproduced; and secondly, on the state of the instruments of reproduction (inheritance law and custom, the labour market, the educational system, etc.), which itself

depends on the state of the power relations between the classes.[35]

This quotation is offered at such length as another reminder of the consistency of Bourdieu's overall theoretical framework. Explicitly or implicitly, it is all here: strategies, the habitus with its dispositions, subjective expectations of objective probabilities and social reproduction. Whether he is talking about the Kabyle struggle for honour, Béarnais marriage strategies or the symbolic violence of French education or cultural consumption, Bourdieu is concerned with the same issues: the manner in which the routine practices of individual actors are determined, at least in large part, by the history and objective structure of their existing social world, and how, inasmuch as the nature of that social world is taken to be axiomatic, those practices contribute – without this being their intention – to the maintenance of its existing hierarchical structure. To appropriate a distinction originally formulated by Raymond Firth, social organisation may change but social structure remains relatively constant.[36] This is the key to understanding Bourdieu's notion of 'competitive struggle':

> the form of class struggle which the dominated classes allow to be imposed on them when they accept the stakes offered by the dominant classes. It is an integrative struggle and, by virtue of the initial handicaps, a reproductive struggle, since those who enter this chase, in which they are beaten before they start. . .implicitly recognize the legitimacy of the goals pursued by those whom they pursue, by the mere fact of taking part.[37]

Having constituted 'objective classes' by occupation, and related these to 'constructed classes' which are positioned in social space by the volume and composition of their mixture of economic and cultural capital, Bourdieu adds to this the relationship between class habitus and life-style(s). Here the body and its hexis are of great importance, particularly in areas such as cuisine, sport, clothes and non-verbal communication. Schematically, the underlying model is as follows: (a) objective *conditions of existence* combine with *position* in social structure to produce (b) the *habitus*, 'a structured and structuring structure', which consists of (c) a 'system of schemes *generating* classifiable practices and works' and (d) a 'system of schemes of perception and appreciation' or *taste*, which between them produce (e) 'classifiable *practices and works*', resulting in (f) a *life-style*, 'a system of classified and classifying practices, i.e. distinctive signs'.[38] While there may be quite a distance between the first and last instances, the determinism of this scheme is unmistakable.

There are as many fields of preferences as there are fields of stylistic possibilities. It is taste which mediates the correspondence between classes of products and classes of consumers, in a relationship of 'elective affinity'. Each field of possibilities – be it popular music or gardening – offers a sufficient range of relationships of similarity and dissimilarity with respect to its products to constitute a 'system of differences' which allows the comprehensive expression of basic social differences (class) and 'well-nigh inexhaustible possibilities for the pursuit of distinction'.[39]

Using a model of social space such as that constructed by Bourdieu – a multidimensional arena in which economic *and* cultural capital are both the objects *and* the weapons of a competitive struggle between classes – allows or holds out the possibility of a reconciliation between competing theories of modern society, between 'theories which describe the social world in the language of stratification and those which speak the language of the class struggle'.[40] This attempt at theoretical synthesis, or, more accurately perhaps, the bringing of two theoretical traditions into creative conflict with each other, may account for the apparent contradiction in *Distinction* between a tight, circular model of social and cultural reproduction, on the one hand, and the fluidity over time of the system of 'competitive struggle', on the other.

This fluidity is nowhere more apparent than in the middle reaches of the system, the petite bourgeoisie. It is, however, within the dominant class, the bourgeoisie, that symbolic struggles are most apparent and most severe. It is here that the definition of Cultural legitimacy is fought over. It is also within the dominant class, according to Bourdieu, that the struggle occurs 'to define the legitimate principles of domination, between economic, educational or social capital'.[41] Here the point is that the dominant class is, in fact, more an uneasy coalition, from the point of view of its members, or a statistical artifact, viewed with the objective gaze of the social survey, than it is a homogeneous social group. Each class fraction has a different combination of economic and cultural capital and a different life-style. Within the overall social space of the dominant class – the bourgeoisie – more of one kind of capital tends to mean less of the other.

The centrepiece of Bourdieu's analysis of the structure of life-styles of the various class fractions is a correspondence analysis of the relationship between various survey items relating to legit-imate Culture, 'middlebrow' culture and ethical dispositions (views, for example, on the nature of friendship), on one side of the calculation, and father's occupation, educational qualifi-cations, income and age, on the other. For legitimate Cultural tastes within the dominant class, for example, this yields a con-tinuum of differentiation with cultural producers and higher edu-cation teachers at one end, executives and engineers intermedi-ately classified, and commercial employers at the other. The closer together class fractions are, the sharper is likely to be the boundary between them in terms of its symbolisation. Not least of all, this reflects the different social trajectories that lie behind present social locations:

> The classification struggle which is waged initially within firms, a struggle for supremacy between production and publicity, between engineering and marketing. . .and all the similar struggles which are fought out within the dominant fraction of the dominant class, are inseparable from conflicts of values which involve the participant's whole world views and arts of living, because they oppose not only different sectional interests but different scholastic and occupational careers and, through them, different social recruitment areas and therefore ultimate differences in habitus.[42]

Different class fractions, in addition to their engagement in the struggles of the moment ('sectional interests'), also have different collective histories: their social and historical roots are different. The old and the new, the established and the *arriviste*, compete in the struggle over the possession of, and the relationship between, 'temporal and spiritual powers'.[43]

The notion of social trajectories – ideal typical in the case of collectivities and categories, to some extent empirical for indi-viduals – is of importance to Bourdieu's understanding of class. Time and its passage is located at the heart of the analysis, in the form of individual and collective histories. However, equally important is the implication of the past and the present in the likelihood of a future: an 'objective probability'. The notion of a trajectory involves description and prediction: each might be thought to determine the other.

This aspect of Bourdieu's model of social class is perhaps at its clearest in his discussion of the petite bourgeoisie. They are in the intermediate location reserved for social categories – class fractions – which are either rising or falling in the field of class relations. In this area of uncertainty the key to the game is 'cultural goodwill' and what is at stake is their *knowledge* of Culture rather than their *acknowledgement* of it. It goes without saying, for the petit bourgeois, that Culture – however it might be defined – is a 'good thing':

> The whole relationship of the petite bourgeoisie to cul-
> ture can in a sense be deduced from the considerable
> gap between knowledge and recognition, the source of
> the cultural goodwill which takes different forms depend-
> ing on the degree of familiarity with legitimate culture,
> that is, on social origin and the associated mode of cul-
> tural acquisition.[44]

This cultural goodwill manifests itself as a 'cultural docility', a sense of 'unworthiness', a 'reverence' for Culture. It is an 'avidity combined with anxiety', the product of 'undifferentiated rever-ence', which leads the petit bourgeois to mistake Gilbert and Sullivan for 'serious' music, or educational television programmes for science. In their relation to Culture, the petite bourgeoisie transforms whatever it latches onto into 'middle-brow' culture: 'legitimate culture is not made for him (and is often made against him), so that he is not made for it . . . it ceases to be what it is as soon as he appropriates it'.[45] If the legitimate gaze of the bourgeoisie bestows legitimacy, the middle-brow gaze of the petit bourgeois imparts a charming mediocrity to all that it recognises.

The petite bourgeoisie is, however, if anything even more internally differentiated than the dominant bourgeoisie: there are the autodidacts, the anti-intellectual small shopkeepers and the upwardly mobile managers who defer their own social and cul-tural gratification in an investment strategy aimed at securing a bourgeois future for their children. Each has a different place in Bourdieu's social map of the varieties of petit bourgeois taste.

He also offers a solution to the minor puzzle, posed in Chapter Five, about what happened to those for whom the expansion of higher education in the 1960s created a disjuncture between their subjective expectations and their objective probabilities. The answer seems to be that they become social workers. Those who are unable to find appropriately bourgeois employment, and for whom family and educational background encourage a view of themselves as an 'ethical vanguard', move into the occupational niches between the teaching and medical professions. A range of 'cultural reconversion' strategies result in a 'profession of faith' ending up as a profession. This is allied to a rejection or inversion of the 'ascetic morality of the established petite bourgeoisie', an embracement of alternatives which becomes a celebration of what it appears to reject:

> Classified, déclassés, aspiring to a higher class, they see themselves as unclassifiable, 'excluded', 'dropped out', 'marginal', anything rather than categorized, assigned to a class, a determinate place in social space. And yet all of their practices . . . speak of classification – but in the mode of denial . . . [They are] thinly disguised expressions of a sort of dream of social flying, a desperate attempt to defy the gravity of the social field . . . these new intellectuals are inventing an art of living which provides them with the gratifications and prestige of the intellectual at the least cost . . .[46]

And there is much more in this delightful vein. It may simply be that Bourdieu is appealing to my own prejudices in this case, but his analysis of the new 'caring' professions is a timely reminder of his undoubted capacity, *despite* the serious problems which exist with respect to his general theory, to hit the nail on the head as an empirical sociologist. The more enthusiasm with which an alternative way is espoused, the more securely is the mainstream defined and signposted, and the principles upon which it is founded reproduced.

From the resentment of the displaced intellectuals of the stranded, counter-cultural petite bourgeoisie, Bourdieu moves on to the 'choice of the necessary' which he characterises as the working-class relation to culture. His argument here can be briefly put. Economic constraints and the dispositions of the working-class habitus produce an adaptive response which is distinguished by the relative absence of aesthetic choice-making: 'nothing is more alien to working-class women than the typically bourgeois idea of making each object in the home the occasion for an aesthetic choice.'[47] This is not just because they cannot *afford* aesthetic sensitivites. Bourdieu is emphatic that income only produces choices – or their refusal – in conjunction with a habitus that is already in harmony with the economic limitations within which it functions (and of which, historically, it is a product). The last refuge of working-class cultural autonomy, he goes on to argue, lies in the 'values of virility', the 'decisive point of relation to the body' which is rooted in a history of manual labour and is under threat from social and economic change. The dominated class, in danger of coming to see themselves *completely* through the mediation of the dominant definition of the body, are in a poor position to resist inasmuch as hexis, 'the most fundamental principle of class unity and identity', is located in the unconscious and, hence, not easily available for mobilisation in organised and knowing resistance.[48]

Within the working class there is, of course, also differentiation. Bourdieu calls the cultural and political differences between skilled workers and foremen, who remain typical of their class, and office workers, already in the race for mobility, a 'real frontier'. Where the former watch sports and the circus on television, the latter view educational programmes. More generally, however, it is in culture – a way of life that is characterised by a 'realistic (but not resigned) hedonism' and 'sceptical (but not cynical) materialism' – rather than politics that whatever working-class unity and solidarity *is* to be found *can* be found. The working-class habitus is both an adaptation to the realities of working-class life and a defence against them.[49]

The cultural dispossession which Bourdieu attributes to the working class is also manifest in their attitude towards politics. In an argument which harks back to his earliest days in Algeria (see Chapter Two), he argues that abstentionism and the large number of people who answer 'don't know' in political opinion polls are to be found disproportionately among the working class. As such they are vital to the reproduction of the established order and the maintenance of the illusion of liberal democracy (which is, of course, the political equivalent of meritocracy and equal opportunity). The possession of a 'personal opinion' on matters political is related to class and is constructed by class relations. 'Indifference', says Bourdieu, 'is only a manifestation of impotence.'[50] The readiness to speak or act politically – even only to the limited extent of casting a vote – reflects the sense of having the *right* to speak or act. This sense of right – an analogue, no doubt of the sense of distinction – is related to a sense of competence:

> The authorized speech of status-generated competence, a powerful speech which helps to create what it says, is answered by the silence of an equally status-linked incompetence, which is experienced as technical incapacity and leaves no choice but delegation . . .[51]

Political competence – self-defined – is related to class position and the trajectory of probabilities attached to it. This 'status competence' both entitles and requires the bearer to engage in political action, however modest. It only exists, however, for those whose trajectories permit its perception as 'realistic'. For the working class, realism dictates a drawing back from personal opinion, a polite equivocation or concession to what is thought to be expected in response to the pollster's questions: it is 'nothing to do with me' or 'won't make any difference anyway'. Thus do the middle and upper reaches of the class system dominate the production of 'general opinion' (which, in its turn, feeds back into the discourse and opinion of actors, the working class being disproportionately vulnerable to such influence).

Bourdieu's central argument in *Distinction* is that struggles about the meaning of things, and specifically the meaning of the social world, are an aspect of class struggle. In this respect it is essentially the same argument as *Reproduction*: the social reproduction of the established order is largely secured by symbolic violence, a process of cultural reproduction. Although it is less deterministic in its depiction of the workings of the system – fluidity and change are documented – the underlying general theory remains the same and so do the problems. Social and cultural reproduction models of society seem, of necessity perhaps, to involve the importation of determinism.

More specifically, the analysis remains weak, for example, at the institutional level. The discussion of the rise of the 'caring' professions, while incisive and thoughtful, says nothing about the manner in which this has occurred within an institutional framework of state welfare provision, nor about the relationship of many such professions to institutional social control. Similarly, as Garnham has pointed out, the institutions of cultural production – the 'culture industry' – are more or less completely neglected by Bourdieu.[52] And so on: all of the critical comments which may have wearied the reader by their reiteration could be made here, albeit perhaps less forcefully.

There are also, however, particular problems with *Distinction*.

In terms of method, the analysis of the relationship between life-styles and class fractions is flawed – and it is a flaw which lies at the heart of the study. Class fractions are defined in terms of occupation and employment status. Life-styles, however, are not immediately self-evident. Their constituent practices are scattered across a variety of different fields. As a consequence, their coherence, the 'reality' of their existence, is concealed. How then is their hidden unity to be discovered? Some sort of extraneous classificatory device is needed to sort out the population in order that the clusters of practices and tastes which cohere as the life-styles of categories of the population may reveal themselves. Simply using class fraction – occupation – to sort out the sample would be likely to render the argument somewhat circular. Bourdieu appears to be aware of this problem; instead of class fraction he uses a combination of father's occupation, education, income and age. However, the first three of these, in particular, are likely to be related to occupation (class fraction) in a systematic and positive fashion. It is, therefore, not surprising that different class fractions exhibit distinct life-styles inasmuch as the basis for the analytical classification of research subjects as members of either life-styles or class fractions is similar.[53]

The problem could perhaps have been avoided by allocating life-style identities to subjects on the basis of either patterns of social interaction[54] or self-identification.[55] The reader is left uncertain about the social meaning of the bundles of practices and attributes identified as 'life-styles', and the relationships they have with each other. The question of the relationship between class and life-style (status group) also remains unresolved. Is it 'real' or an artifact of the analysis?

On a different tack, I am less convinced than Bourdieu – and I am similarly sceptical about *Homo Academicus* – that the use of French data does not undermine the general relevance of the argument. It may be that there is, for example, something highly specific about the relationship of the French metropolitan elite to Culture. America or Britain may be very different.

Next, the superficiality of his treatment of the working class is matched only by its condescension. Does Bourdieu *really* believe that it is alien to working-class women to furnish and decorate their homes on the basis of aesthetic choices? As Mary Douglas has pointed out, his own evidence suggests that working-class people seem no less concerned to make distinctions than anyone else.[56] Perhaps it is time he dusted off his anthropologist's hat and went out and spent some time among the people about whom he writes. In this, as in many other aspects of the book, he betrays his membership of French bourgeois cultural networks. Despite his good intentions, this elevated point of view taints the entire discussion with the sub-text of the author's own distinction (and that of its intended audience).

Finally, and it is also an issue which has been raised by other commentators,[57] although Bourdieu is obviously correct in his rejection of a Kantian transcendent aesthetic, it may be less obvious that his own approach is, in its own way, no less reductionist. Culture and taste are, for Bourdieu, wholly arbitrary: history and social construction are all. Leaving aside the matter of whether aesthetic response may in some way be innate, the question of the role of individual psychology in the creation of taste and aesthetic preference has some significance, if only insofar as it may help to account for the non-conformist aesthetic impulse. So too does the sense of history as the *longue durée*: how in Bourdieu's scheme are we to understand, for example, the rise of modernism? As in the rest of Bourdieu's work, conformism is of the essence. There is little room for innovation or deviance except insofar as they represent limited manoeuvres within an overall framework of stability.

Despite the generally critical tone of the discussion so far, and despite the difficulty of the language Bourdieu employs and the complexity of the presentation, *Distinction* is a truly impressive piece of sociology. As an exploration of the place of Culture (and culture) in modern industrial society, what it has to say is indispensable. The pursuit of distinction is also one of the themes of *Homo Academicus*, particularly the role of language use in the status-seeking strategies of academics. We shall examine this theme further in the next chapter.

NOTES AND REFERENCES

[1] P. Bourdieu, *Distinction: A Social Critique of the Judgement of Taste*, London, Routledge and Kegan Paul (1984), p. 5.
[2] P. Bourdieu, *In Other Words*, Cambridge, Polity (1990), p. 22.
[3] B.S. Turner, *Status*, Milton Keynes, Open University Press (1988), p. 66.

[4] P. Bourdieu, L. Boltanski, R. Castel and J.C. Chamboredon, *Photography: A Middle-brow Art*, Cambridge, Polity (1990).

[5] *Ibid.*, p. 7.

[6] *Ibid.*, p. 21.

[7] *Ibid.*, p. 60.

[8] *Ibid.*, p. 65.

[9] *Ibid.*, p. 72.

[10] *Ibid.*, pp. 95–8.

[11] *Ibid.*, p. 96.

[12] P. Bourdieu, A. Darbel, with D. Schnapper, *The Love of Art: European Art Museums and their Public*, Cambridge, Polity (1991).

[13] *Ibid.*, p. 108.

[14] *Ibid.*, p. 40.

[15] *Ibid.*, p. 109.

[16] *Ibid.*, p. 110.

[17] *Ibid.*, p. 111.

[18] P. Bourdieu, 'Intellectual Field and Creative Project', in M.F.D. Young (ed.), *Knowledge and Control: New Directions in the Sociology of Education*, London, Collier-Macmillan (1971), p. 161.

[19] There are, in fact, some areas of overlap between the two texts: compare, for example, *Photography*, *op. cit.*, pp. 95–7, with 'Intellectual Field and Creative Project', *op. cit.*, pp. 175–6.

[20] P. Bourdieu, 'Intellectual Field and Creative Project', *op. cit.*, p. 161.

[21] *Ibid.*, p. 163.

[22] *Ibid.*, pp. 166–7.

[23] *Ibid.*, p. 170.

[24] *Ibid.*, pp. 170–3.

[25] *Ibid.*, p. 182.

[26] *Ibid.*, p. 183.

[27] V.L. Zolberg, 'Taste as a Social Weapon', *Contemporary Sociology*, vol. 15 (1986), p. 511.

[28] P. Bourdieu, *Distinction*, *op. cit.*, p. 100.

[29] N. Bryson, *Vision and Painting: The Logic of the Gaze*, London, Macmillan (1983), p. 162.

[30] P. Bourdieu, *Distinction*, *op. cit.*, p.xii.

[31] *Ibid.*, p. 54.

[32] *Ibid.*, p. 56.

[33] *Ibid.*, p. 101.

[34] *Ibid.*, pp. 128–9.

[35] *Ibid.*, p. 125.

[36] R. Firth, *Essays on Social Organization and Values*, London, Athlone Press (1964), pp. 30–87.

[37] P. Bourdieu, *Distinction, op. cit.*, p. 165.

[38] *Ibid.*, p. 171.

[39] *Ibid.*, p. 226.

[40] *Ibid.*, p. 245.

[41] *Ibid.*, p. 254.

[42] *Ibid.*, pp. 309–10.

[43] *Ibid.*, pp. 315–17.

[44] *Ibid.*, p. 319.

[45] *Ibid.*, p. 327.

[46] *Ibid.*, p. 370.

[47] *Ibid.*, p. 379.

[48] *Ibid.*, p. 384.

[49] *Ibid.*, pp. 386–96.

[50] *Ibid.*, p. 406.

[51] *Ibid.*, p. 413.

[52] N. Garnham, 'Extended review: Bourdieu's *Distinction*', *Sociological Review*, vol. 34 (1986), p. 432.

[53] In my original review of *Distinction* for the journal *Sociology*, vol. 20 (1986), pp. 103–5, I make this basic criticism in a different form to that which is offered here; my understanding of what Bourdieu was doing was slightly incorrect (although my complaint remains valid).

[54] See, for example: A. Stewart, K. Prandy and R. Blackburn, *Social Stratification and Occupations*, London, Macmillan (1980).

[55] See, for example: R. Jenkins, *Lads, Citizens and Ordinary Kids: Working-class Youth Life-styles in Belfast*, London, Routledge and Kegan Paul (1983).

[56] M. Douglas, *In the Active Voice*, London, Routledge and Kegan Paul (1982), p. 131.

[57] N. Garnham, 'Extended review', *op. cit.*, pp. 432–3.

7

Uses of Language

Culture, the focus of the previous chapters, is unthinkable without language. The one presupposes the other. This is the conventional sociological and anthropological view, to which Bourdieu subscribes in the strongest possible terms. He insists that language cannot be analysed or understood in isolation from its cultural context and the social conditions of its production and reception. So the first thing to note about the papers on language which he wrote during the 1970s and 1980s, a selection of which have recently been published in *Language and Symbolic Power*,[1] is that they are a critique of pure, formalist linguistics, most obviously the work of Saussure and and Chomsky. In particular, he objects to Saussure's distinction between *langue* (language) and *parole* (speech), and Chomsky's differentiation between 'competence' and 'performance'. Each depends on the methodological constitution of an abstract domain of language – simultaneously 'real' and 'ideal' – which is drawn upon in the production of mundane written or spoken language in all of its variety.

He argues that uniform, linguistic communities of the kind which these linguistic models imply do not exist. 'Standard languages', such as they are, are the product of complex social processes, generally bound up with a history of state formation, and are simply one version of a language – and a socially highly specific one at that. They are not *the* language. Moreover, this kind of linguistic analysis 'freezes' language, creates it as 'structure'. This, the grammarian's view of language, is analogous to the reified view of social reality which is produced by the detachment of objectivist social science – both are concerned with the generation of *rules* – which Bourdieu has criticised elsewhere (see Chapter Three).

In the second place, Bourdieu's writings on language are an extension to a new empirical topic of the theoretical approach which he has developed in his anthropological work and in his studies of education and cultural consumption. He thinks 'that the division between linguistics and sociology is unfortunate and deleterious to both disciplines'.[2] Since language is intrinsically a social and practical phenomenon it is fair game for sociologists. More than that, the analysis of communication and discourse should constitute one of the foundation stones of the sociological enterprise. Nor does Bourdieu see his analyses of language, education and cultural consumption as separate enterprises: they are all concerned with the manner in which domination is achieved by the manipulation of symbolic and cultural resources and with the collusion of the dominated.

Bourdieu has also, in *Homo Academicus* and *The Political Ontology of Martin Heidegger*, discussed the linguistic practices of academics and their place in the competition for cultural distinction. In this chapter I will first outline briefly Bourdieu's sociology of language. I will then move on to discuss academic language use. Finally, drawing on both of these areas of his work, I will look at Bourdieu's own use of language.

'ORDINARY' LANGUAGE

For Bourdieu, all speech acts are the outcome of two 'causal series'. First, there is the habitus, the 'linguistic habitus' which encompasses the cultural propensity to say particular things, a specific linguistic competence (the capacity to 'speak properly') and the social capacity to use that competence appropriately. Second, there is the 'linguistic market', which takes the form of sanctions and censorships, and which defines what *cannot* be said as much as what *can*. Bourdieu is thus concerned with linguistic practices from the point of view of their production *and* their reception: the speech act is not to be reduced to 'mere execution'.

Given that language is thus firmly situated, for Bourdieu, within social relationships and interaction, the rest of his general theoretical framework comes into play in understanding discourse:

> linguistic relations are always relations of power (*rapports de force*) and, consequently, cannot be elucidated within the compass of linguistic analysis alone. Even the simplest linguistic exchange brings into play a complex and ramifying web of historical power relations between the speaker, endowed with a specific social authority, and an audience, which recognizes this authority to varying degrees, as well as between the groups to which they respectively belong.[3]

In this encounter between the linguistic habitus and the market for its products, it is the speaker's *anticipation* of the reception which his/her discourse will receive (its 'price') which contributes to *what* is said and *how*. Thus it is the actor's subjective expectations of the probabilities of the situation which produce self-censorship. This is one root of the inequalities of linguistic competence which characterise human communication.

Processes of nation-building produce a unified linguistic market in which price and profit – the intersection of production and reception – are neither locally nor situationally determined. In this context, and indeed more generally perhaps, linguistic differences are the 'retranslation' of social differences: linguistic markets are, therefore, heavily implicated in specific fields. The dominant legitimate language is a distinct capital which, in discourse, produces, as its profit, a sense of the speaker's distinction. It is this distinction, along with legitimate correctness, which constitutes excellence in language.[4] The relationship between dominant (nationally legitimate) and dominated (situationally specific) discourses is the same competitive struggle that takes place with respect to other cultural products. The unequal distribution of linguistic capital which provides this struggle with its object, its weapons and its framework, is an aspect of the class system, as mediated by formal education:[5] 'utterances are not only (save in exceptional circumstances) signs to be understood and deciphered; they are also *signs of wealth* intended to be evaluated and appreciated, and *signs of authority*, intended to be believed and obeyed'.[6]

Speech and other forms of discourse are, therefore, practical interventions in social life, which have effects and which help to constitute and shape social life. They are both means and ends in processes of symbolic violence and structures of symbolic domination. In this respect, Bourdieu, while acknowledging its influence upon his thinking, is critical of Austin's well known theory of 'performative utterances'.[7] Austin's notion that words which are endowed with 'illocutionary force' possess in themselves the capacity to produce effects is, argues Bourdieu, incorrect. The power of words to *do* things is a function of the authority and appropriateness of their speaker, not to mention the appropriateness of audience and context. The power of words is, if you like, socially constructed in the conditions of their reception and authorisation.[8] But the essential point is that words *do* have power.

Naming and processes of categorisation – and, indeed language in general – thus play an important part in the social construction of reality. Classification is, as we have seen already, central to the social order and to the struggles which are routine within that order. This is of particular significance in the social constitution of groups:

> The transition from the state of being a practical group to the state of being an instituted group (class, nation, etc.) presupposes the construction of the principle of classification capable of producing the set of distinctive properties which characterize the set of members in this group . . .[9]

Here, once again, we have the movement from a class-in-itself (a social category) to a class-for-itself (a group). Bourdieu is also concerned here to highlight what he refers to as the 'theory effect' in advanced societies, the symbolic effectiveness with which institutionalised, codified knowledge – such as, for example, theories of class struggle – intervene in the social conditions which give rise to them. This 'theory effect' is at its most potent when there is a correspondence between 'reality' and the classifications which the theory proposes.[10]

Finally, Bourdieu talks about censorship. This is a familiar theme from his writings on symbolic violence and cultural reproduction. It is the nature and structure of social fields which determines what can and cannot be said. It is via the sanctions of the social arena in question that censorship is effected. The more effective this censorship is, the less apparent it becomes and the more it appears as the axiomatic, natural 'way of the world' of *doxa*:

> The need for this censorship to manifest itself in the form of explicit prohibitions, imposed and sanctioned by an institutionalized authority, diminishes as the mechanisms which ensure the allocation of agents to different positions . . . are increasingly capable of ensuring that the different positions are occupied by agents able and inclined to engage in discourse . . . which is compatible with the objective definition of the position.[11]

The more the system is occupied and worked by those who believe in the system, the less censorship there needs to be. This might be paraphrased by saying that the ultimate success of censorship – which, let us remember, is about what people *think* as well as about what they *say* – is to be found in its apparent abolition. Some things become impossible to say or, if said, they are impossible to take seriously. The cultural arbitrary is legitimated and accepted not only as the 'way things are', but as the way they *ought* to be. This state of affairs is founded upon the fit between the subjectivity of the habitus and the objective nature of the field or social space and its structure of positions:

> formally correct comprehension would remain purely formal and empty if it were not often a cover for an understanding at once deeper and more obscure, the entente established on the basis of an affinity of the *habitus* and a more or less perfect homology of positions.[12]

Far from being an 'original, innovative approach to linguistic phenomena'[13] this is basically the modification by Bourdieu's general theoretical scheme of the current sociolinguistic conventional wisdom, which sees language as a variable social phenomenon, competences in which are socially defined, unevenly distributed and valorised, and rooted in hierarchically structured communication contexts.[14] Bourdieu's critique of formal linguistics is, in fact, old hat. Inasmuch as it is an allotrope of his general theory and, specifically, of his theories of social reproduction and symbolic violence, it is vulnerable to most of the criticisms which have been advanced in earlier chapters. Most particularly, despite his initial emphasis upon linguistic variation within a marketplace, Bourdieu's eventual position suggests a view of language (and thought) which is more homogeneous and conformist – as a result of censorship, whether it be self-censorship, overt institutional censorship or the hidden censorship of *doxa* – than anything else. Words have power in Bourdieu's world, but that power seems only to flow in one direction.

ACADEMIC LANGUAGE

Language, then, according to Bourdieu, is an intrinsic element of the competitive struggles over the use of culture and of the processes of cultural reproduction which make such an important contribution to the social reproduction of the established order. It is, however, only within the context of a specific field that language is used; it is to that context that, in any given case, it owes the specificities of its voice and its resonance. It will speak more loudly, and to greater effect, in some fields than in others.

In the academic field, the use of language is one of the most significant modes of struggle: words are both currency and commodity in the academic marketplace. Academic struggles appear to be about two related things. First, the issue of legitimacy and cultural distinction is at the heart of the collective enterprise:

> the university field is, like any other, the locus of a struggle to determine the conditions and criteria of legitimate membership and legitimate hierarchy . . . the different sets of individuals (more or less constituted into groups) who are defined by these different criteria have a vested interest in them.[15]

The vested interest comes from the prime business of the academic field, i.e. the production of intellectually classified and legitimately categorised agents. This, of necessity, involves both classifiers – who owe their own authority to classify, at least in part, to their own status as classified products of the field – and classified. The classification of the classifiers is not a once-and-for-all *imprimateur*, however. The field of academia is a market wherein the stock of reputation and status falls and rises throughout an individual's career as a consequence of its valorisation or not by the informal and formal processes of peer-group evaluation and institutional hierarchical consecration.

What is at stake, therefore, for the classifying agents – professors and lecturers – is reputation and its ongoing maintenance and enhancement: 'There are surely few social worlds where power depends so strongly on belief, where it is so true that, in the words of Hobbes, "Reputation of power is power".'[16] Reputation is, therefore, symbolic capital – which is, in the right contexts, translatable into other kinds of capital – within the academic field. The French academic is no different, in this respect, to the Kabyle peasant in the urgency and subtlety of his pursuit of honour (and, yes, it usually is a 'him'). One specific characteristic of the academic field, however, is that there are different kinds of honorific reputation available: the *internal*, which while dependent upon a particular kind of bureaucratised intellectual production also involves the work of administration etc., and the *external*, which depends upon international intellectual reputation, public activities, etc. Academic power is most usually related to the former.[17] Of whichever kind, however, reputation depends upon the use of words.

The second thing which serves to provide the academic field with its distinctive character is the role of what Bourdieu has called, following Sartre, 'bad faith'. At its simplest, this means doing one thing while saying or thinking another. It is strongly implied, however, that this is an unconscious manoeuvre which permits people to do things to which they might not wish to admit, especially to themselves. It is thus a form or a constituent of the processes of misrecognition which, in Bourdieu's eyes, pervade social life.

There seem to be at least two different kinds of bad faith revealed in his studies of academic life. First, there is 'the rejection of the inaccessible' or 'the choice of the inevitable'.[18] Academics adjust their ambitions and goals so that they end up only 'wanting' what the field realistically offers them. This, however, inasmuch as it is a restatement of Bourdieu's notion of the subjective expectation of objective probabilities, suggests that bad faith is the dominant motor of history and practice (which, of course, it may be). The other kind of bad faith is more a property of the system or the field, and it is here in particular that misrecognition is significant. It is something which has already been discussed in Chapter Five. Bourdieu is concerned with the way in which social judgements and classifications are systematically translated into academic or intellectual judgements. This allows the legitimacy of the academic field, its processes and its products to be maintained: social reproduction is misrecognised as meritocracy. The whole system is, in this sense, founded upon bad faith. An extension or transposition of this second variety of bad faith, from the functioning of the field to the practice of individual agents occupying positions within it, might be the masking of the pursuit of symbolic capital (reputation and distinction) as disinterested scholarship and intellectual endeavour.

How does language and its use figure in the competitive struggles for distinction and the collective bad faith of the academic field? To look at strategies for the accumulation of honour and reputation first, Bourdieu alludes – sometimes only in passing – to a variety of ways of speaking which are important. There are those which are designed to enhance one's own capital. The adoption of an 'elevated style' is one such device:

> It is through the 'elevated' style that the status of a discourse is invoked, as is the respect due to that status. One does not react to a sentence such as this, 'the real dwelling plight lies in this that mortals ever search anew for the nature of dwelling, that they must ever learn to dwell', in the same way that one would react to a statement in ordinary language, such as this: 'the housing shortage is getting worse' . . .[19]

Elsewhere Bourdieu suggests that literary distinction – and social science and other academic writing remains, no matter how much its authors may strive to disguise the fact, literary production of a sort – is bound up with distance from day-to-day language: 'Value always arises from deviation, *deliberate or not*, with respect to the most widespread usage'.[20] This is, arguably, a dimension of 'elevated style'.

A related tactic which may be adopted is the production of an 'illusion of independence' from 'ordinary language' – and, by strong implication, *ordinary thought* – by 'staging an artificial break' with it.[21] Words and linguistic structures become transformed, by the specificities of their definition, context and use in academic discourse, so that what appears to mean one thing – in 'ordinary' discourse – turns out to mean another or, more subtly, hint at a whole string of hitherto unsuspected allusions. This appropriation of language 'produces the illusion of systematic order, and, through the break with ordinary language thus effected, the illusion of an autonomous system'.[22] In the context of his critique of Heidegger, he describes this as a 'process of distortion, worthy of the conjuror who draws attention to something unimportant in order to distract our attention from what he has to hide'.[23]

On the other hand, there are tactics which are designed to enhance one's own reputation and distinction at the expense of another's, be that person a living peer or an intellectual ancestor. Bourdieu mentions three such ways of talking. First, there is 'labelling', which he characterises as a subtle, or not so subtle, mode of academic abuse. We have already seen, in Chapter One, that he considers the question of whether someone is a Marxist or a Weberian to be almost always polemical and threatening. Labelling – whether it be one's categorisation as a 'functionalist', 'determinist', 'Marxist', 'structuralist', 'rational action theorist', or whatever – is, says Bourdieu, 'the "scholarly" equivalent of the insult . . . and all the more powerful the more the label is . . . both more of a stigma and more imprecise, thus irrefutable'.[24] In the same passage – which is an irritated response to Burger's critique of his work on the literary field – Bourdieu points to another verbal weapon, the subtle use of qualifiers (such as, in the case of Burger's comments, 'exclusively' and 'merely' added in strategic places) to characterise someone's work as more simple, and more simple-minded, than it is. The critic is spared the necessity of a detailed critique, while the victim is left to respond to an attack which derives much of its force from its relatively insubstantial elusiveness.

Finally, there is the way in which scholars relate to their forebears. Because there is actually very little new under the sun, and inasmuch as academic distinction implies a degree of distinctiveness, this may pose something of a problem. What is the appropriate stance to adopt? Legitimacy requires some kind of location within a consecrated tradition. On the other hand, distinction entails a claim to be saying something new and different. Bourdieu does little more than hint at this:

> The philosophical genealogy which the philosopher claims for himself in his retrospective interpretations is a well-founded fiction. The inheritor of a learned tradition always refers to his predecessors or his contemporaries in the very distance he adopts towards them.[25]

He goes on to say that this 'fictional' positioning with respect to the field of possible stances – the tradition – is also an adoption of a stance with respect to 'politico-moral' possibilities. Most illuminating, from the point of view of our discussion, is Bourdieu's characterisation of the creation of a professional or intellectual identity as a *negative* process of distancing – rather than one of *positive* identification – with respect to the ideas and discourse of others.

The art of euphemism is another characteristic aspect of academic discourse. It provides us with the most obvious bridge between the pursuit of distinction and the exercise of bad faith. At its most basic, there is the 'ordinary process of euphemization' which: 'substitutes one word (often of contradictory meaning) for another, or visibly neutralizes the ordinary meaning either by an explicit caution (inverted commas, for instance) or by a distinctive definition. . .'.[26] Leaving aside whether what Bourdieu is describing here can really be thought as euphemisation, this is an aspect of the subversion of 'ordinary' language, as discussed above.

More important – and this has also been considered earlier – is the central role of euphemism in academic bad faith (and here we are concerned with the most precise use of words). In the 'Postscript' to *Homo Academicus*[27] Bourdieu turns his spotlight on the 'categories of professorial judgement': the way in which words which apparently *say* one thing (about intellectual ability or academic style) actually *mean* another (denoting social status and endowment of cultural capital). This effect operates whether it is students or colleagues who are being judged and the carefully weighted euphemism is the primary device through which the duality of judgements is communicated. Thus is bad faith exercised in good faith:

> It is no doubt through the medium of the successive *classifications* which have made them what they are . . . that the classified producers of the academic system, pupils or professors, have acquired . . . their practical mastery of classificatory systems, adjusted circumstantially to objective classes, which allow them to classify everything – starting with themselves – according to academic taxonomies, and which function within each one of them – in all good faith and genuine belief – as a machine for transforming social classifications into academic classifications, as recognized – yet – misconstrued social classifications.[28]

Because of the snug fit between the academic habitus and the structure of the academic field, the euphemism, in masking the reality of social reproduction, *becomes* or *produces* that reality. What is categorised as 'dull and pedestrian' becomes so (and vice versa for the 'interesting and confidant').

In order, therefore, to understand the role of language in the struggles of the academic field, both its production and its reception must be considered. This is in the very nature of processes of classification and judgement. Bourdieu himself is, of course, an academic, involved in the same struggles, and as dependent on using language for his achievements within them as any other academic. It is to this that we will now turn.

BOURDIEU'S LANGUAGE

Bourdieu paints a picture of academia – a social world that is, more than most, dominated by the use of language – which is anything but edifying. It is also regrettably convincing, although French universities *may* be more extreme in this respect than similar institutions in the Anglophone world. In constructing his analysis he has, in addition, provided us with a framework for examining his own intellectual and academic enterprise. There are at least three reasons for doing so, the first of which is that he invites us to. His persistent arguments for a reflexive social science suggest no other alternative:

> if the sociology I propose differs in any significant way from the other sociologies of the past and of the present, it is above all in that it *continually turns back onto itself the scientific weapons it produces*.[29]

In this sense, a sociology of Bourdieu's sociology should be understood as an example of the 'objectification of objectification' in practice.

A second reason is that, in writing about French academia, he is of necessity proferring an analysis of the social world within which he works. Logic would suggest that, unless he is in some sense different from his peers (and his successful career implies that he could not be *too* deviant), this analysis should also be applicable to him. Fair play, if nothing else, suggests that we should examine him under his own spotlight.

Finally, there is a problem – certainly for this reader – with the language which Bourdieu uses. As I have already said in

Chapter One, I do not think that his use of language – his choice of words and his overall style – is in any way entailed by the nature or complexity of his substantive subject matter or his theory. I hope that this point has been made inasmuch as I have been able to summarise and discuss his work, in a language which is considerably simpler and clearer than his, without doing his ideas a disservice.[30] I leave that to the reader to decide. However, the question is still posed: *why* does Bourdieu write in the way that he does?

Before attempting to answer this question, some further preliminary comments are perhaps due, even at the risk of anticipating the discussion below. In the first place the pursuit of distinction is not in itself reprehensible. Bourdieu's sociology suggests that most, if not all, of us do it and I don't see any reason to argue with him. Certainly, two of the considerations which brought me, for example, to write this book were the thought of what it might do for my professional reputation and, it must be admitted, vanity – I was flattered to be asked. So, in this respect, I am not, I hope, allowing the mote in Bourdieu's eye to obscure the beam in my own.

Bad faith, however, is another matter. It is also a charge on which it is difficult to secure a convincing conviction. In order successfully to expose a gap between practices, on the one hand, and conscious intentions or unconscious purposes, on the other, the latter must be identifiable. This is rarely easy. In this case I will do no more than compare what Bourdieu does – how he writes and what he says – with what he says *he* is doing and, more to the point perhaps, what he insists that *other* people (doing similar things) are *really* doing. After that the jury will, so to speak, be out.

First of all, then, let us look at Bourdieu's writings insofar as they might be part of a strategy to maintain and enhance his own distinction, reputation and status. He has isolated three aspects of academic discourse which are bound up with strategies of this kind. The first is 'elevated style': long, complicated ways of speaking, a conscious distancing from ordinary language, the idiosyncratic definition of words in contrast to their conventional meaning, etc. Bourdieu's writing is consistently characterised by all of these things, and none of them in a minor way. He has, in fact, described his own literary practice as 'a permanent struggle against ordinary language'.[31] It is a struggle which, needless to say, he generally wins! Although I have consistently tried in this book to use the most straightforward and readily understandable quotations from Bourdieu which I could find – within the limits of appropriateness – even these will, I suspect, serve to make the point. Any reader who requires further convincing is referred to my favourite example of his worst linguistic excesses: the sentence which begins on line five of page xiv of Peter Collier's English translation of *Homo Academicus*. This lasts for sixteen lines, has more than 160 words and is, frankly, an unnecessary monstrosity (not to mention being close to completely unintelligible). And it would not be too difficult to find many other such examples.

Neologisms and apparently technical terms abound in Bourdieu's work. Here, the glosses or explanations which he himself provides often betray their dispensability or redundancy. He talks, for example, about:

> the features of discourse designed to signify the doxic modality of utterances, that is to inspire belief in the truth of what is being said, or on the other hand to point out that it is only a pretence . . .[32]

Given the need to define, at such length, 'the doxic modality of utterances' it is difficult to know *why* the expression was used in the first place, other than as a deliberate signifier of the 'elevated' status of what he is saying. It is not, of course, that a specific, technical language is unnecessary. In sociology and anthropology, as in all specialist discourses – from meteorology to philosophy to plumbing – an appropriately specialist vocabulary is inevitable. In Bourdieu's work, however, one is forced too often to query the communicative necessity of much of the jargon (let alone whether it actually undermines good communication).

Then there is the subversive redefinition of words which already have established meanings. His appropriation of the philosophical term 'habitus' is a very good example of this, as discussed in Chapter Four. In a lecture delivered at the University of San Diego in 1986, he characterised his work as 'constructivist structuralism'. He went on, however, to explain that, here, 'structuralism' did not mean what it usually means (as in the tradition of Saussure or Lévi-Strauss):

> By structuralism or structuralist, I mean that there exist,
> in the social world itself, and not merely in symbolic
> systems, language, myth, etc., objective structures which

are independent of the consciousness and desires of agents and are capable of guiding or constraining their practices or their representations.[33]

'When *I* use a word', said Humpty Dumpty to Alice, 'it means just what I choose it to mean!' The interesting thing, however, is that Bourdieu's redefinition of structuralism here is (a) not in itself particularly radical, and (b) approximates to a definition of what, in Chapter Four, I called 'substantialism'.

It may, of course, be a question of national cultural tradition and writing style: is it that Bourdieu writes the way he does simply because he's French? This may be partly true; certainly the examples of Foucault, Althusser, Lacan, Derrida and Touraine – to light only on the most obvious – would suggest so. Other examples (Braudel, Aron, Boudon, Lefèbvre, even Lévi-Strauss) do not, however, support such a conclusion. If it is a French stylistic tradition, it is far from obligatory. Furthermore, Bourdieu's own work, viewed over time, also suggests otherwise. His writing has become increasingly dense, elliptical and long-winded as his career has progressed. What is more, in interviews he uses language in a much more straightforward and accessible fashion.

Nor does the problem seem to be caused by translation. English language editions of Bourdieu's writings, particularly those which have appeared since the late 1970s, are in every sense *authorised* translations. Not only do we have the translators' testimonies – in various introductory comments – that this is the case, but it is obvious that Bourdieu often seizes upon translation as an opportunity for modification, reformulation and re-presentation. Further, the most cursory comparison with the original texts suggests that the translators do a better than reasonable job of preserving Bourdieu's own voice and style. This is a voice and style which is clearly located within *one* French academic style and one is drawn to the conclusion that this school of academic writing is at least as much concerned with the communication of the author's intellectual distinction and importance as anything else.

Which brings me to the nature of Bourdieu's relation to legitimate intellectual tradition. As we have seen in earlier chapters, 'canonical' authors such as Marx, Weber and Durkheim are there, for Bourdieu, to think *against* as much as anything else. In a different vein, the *Theses on Feuerbach* did not, apparently, influence his thinking; rather, they encouraged him to express his *own* thoughts. His confidence that they were his own thoughts, in this particular case, is striking. Characteristically, Bourdieu adopts one of four positions towards his intellectual ancestors. He either (a) rejects their work outright, (b) agrees with it in part only, (c) recognises its virtues but denies that it has had any influence on him, or (d) mentions them in a throwaway fashion, the very carelessness of which bears all the hallmarks of playful erudition.[34] The latter seems to be particularly favoured in the case of thinkers who are outside Bourdieu's legitimate tradition – novelists, scientists, etc. – and who can, therefore, embroider his distinction without posing a threat. Even his occasional references to the American cartoon heroes, Charlie Brown and Snoopy, can be interpreted in this way.

All four strategies involve a combination of recognition and distancing, and each, in its own way, implies a claim about his own distinction. In the case of structuralism, for example, he is unequivocal in his rejection of it as either a theory or an approach. At the same time, as was demonstrated in Chapter Two, he continues to publish analyses which owe a huge debt to structuralism. Finally, he calls himself a *kind* of structuralist, only to argue that structuralism is something other than its conventional definition would suggest.

This is one aspect of Bourdieu's presentation of himself as a novel and original thinker. In most respects, as I have suggested at various points, this is a spurious claim. It is, however, an important aspect of his broader claim to legitimate distinction and it finds another expression in his depiction and characterisation of rival schools of thought or authors. One often encounters these in his work as straw men, simplified, for the purposes of rhetorical disembowelment, almost beyond recognition. A number of examples spring readily to mind. The model of participant observation which he criticises is, at the very least, an extreme one. Similarly, his depiction, for the purposes of critique, of 'rational action' models of behaviour is partial (in every sense of the word). The same could be said for his characterisations of structuralism and, even more so, existentialism. Sartre, in particular, is nothing like as simple-minded as Bourdieu suggests. Similarly, he can only present himself as offering a significant advance upon Austin's notion of the 'performative utterance' at the expense of a considerable simplification of that notion. Sometimes the simplification is crude; more often it takes the form of selectivity and the subtle use of linguistic devices such as qualifiers.[35] It is, however, always effective.

The illusion of novelty can also be constructed in another way. In a number of key areas of his work Bourdieu simply does not mention pre-existing bodies of work which might be thought to have influenced his thinking. Fredrick Barth, for example, published a seminal and widely acknowledged paper in 1966 which outlines a generative, processual model of social behaviour which bears more than a passing resemblance to aspects of Bourdieu's theory of practice.[36] Similarly, in Barnes' famous original paper on social networks,[37] he uses the metaphor of the 'social field' in a fashion that is, once again, strikingly echoed in Bourdieu's later work. It may well be that neither Barth nor Barnes played any role in his intellectual formation, but it is difficult to imagine that Bourdieu, as an anthropologist, would have been ignorant of their work (although, in a similar vein, he has recently admitted to having made only a very late acquaintanceship with the writings of Gramsci[38]). A more general point, which has already been made in Chapter Three, concerns his lack of engagement with the huge literature on reflexivity in sociological and anthropological research. In the absence of such a discussion, his claim to the construction of a 'reflexive sociology' appears more radical and innovative than it actually is.

There are many ways of paying attention to the work and comments of one's peers. While Bourdieu does not indulge overmuch in the labelling which he so detests – although there can be little doubt of the ferocity with which he identifies some authors, for example, as 'rational action theorists' – there are occasions on which he engages in a style of debate in which, even by the standards of academia, few holds are barred. In *Homo Academicus*, for example, despite an early disclaimer about the need to avoid *ad hominem* polemic in writing about his own professional world,[39] he manages to accuse Raymond Boudon of the 'illicit use of social science', 'exemplary naivety' and self-serving chauvinism, before going on to imply that Boudon has used some of his (Bourdieu's) ideas without acknowledging their source.[40] Elster appears to be another sore point: Bourdieu has, for example, described Elster's *Ulysses and the Sirens* as 'the mediocre remake of a well-known show'.[41] However one might wish to describe Elster, the word 'mediocre' does not come readily to mind.

Elster and Boudon have in common, apart from a certain theoretical affinity, a publicly expressed oppositional stance to Bourdieu, whether intellectual or more strictly political/professional, and this may be a key to understanding the tenor of his remarks about them. Bourdieu's response to criticism is frequently hostile and, it must be said, abusive. When asked, for example, by Wacquant, about criticisms of his work as deterministic – and I must admit here that mine was one of the critiques mentioned – his response was:

> I must say that I find many of these criticisms strikingly superficial; they reveal that those who make them may have paid more attention to the titles of my books (most blatantly in the case of *Reproduction*) than to the actual analyses they contain.[42]

This is not the stuff of constructive academic debate. Whether it reveals massive arrogance or massive insecurity (or both) is beside the point. What Bourdieu is doing here is asserting the power which accrues to his, by now substantial, academic distinction in order to define the position in his own terms and, to resort to one of his own favourite metaphors, run the game his own way. And in that game – which is, by his own analytical admission, a competitive struggle – you are either on his side or playing against him (and, if the latter, not really worth serious attention).

Finally, and this is not something which Bourdieu includes in his catalogue of distinction-oriented strategies of academic literary production, there is the sheer volume of Bourdieu's work. Now this, as all academics will realise, is a double-edged sword – 'never mind the quality feel the width' is a staple theme of senior common room resentment – but, in Bourdieu's case, his productivity has been sufficiently often referred to in a positive and approving vein[43] to qualify its discussion in this context. Bourdieu's *oeuvre* is characterised by an enormous amount of repetition. His essay on the Kabyle house, for example, is reprinted in its entirety in *Algeria 1960* and *The Logic of Practice* and sections of it turn up in *Outline of a Theory of Practice*. Similarly, *The Political Ontology of Martin Heidegger*, following its original publication in *Actes de la recherche en sciences sociales* became, only slightly modified, a book; a large portion of it was also included in *Language and Symbolic Power*. Perhaps the worst example is the re-working of one major book, *Outline of a Theory of Practice* to become, eight years later, another, *The Logic of Practice*, with substantial areas of textual overlap between the two. Bourdieu might choose to defend his publication strategy as a 'work of self-interpretation', 'accomplished in and through the corrections, rectifications, clarifications and refutations through which the author defends his public image'[44] but I am not sure how convincing such a defence would be.

And this brings us, at last, to the issue of bad faith. I have argued that Bourdieu's literary and discursive style can be interpreted as a strategy designed to bolster and generate his own academic and intellectual distinction. He, however, offers a different explanation. If, for example, there is a 'certain vagueness' in some of his concepts – his own example is the concept of the 'field' – this is because they are intentionally 'open' and 'provisional', to permit them to be of maximum heuristic use, and because 'every one of them . . . is, in a condensed form, a research programme and a principle by which one can avoid a whole set of mistakes'.[45]

With specific reference to his refusal to embrace the readability of 'ordinary' language, Bourdieu offers five inter-related justifications for his writing style.[46] First, and perhaps most straightforward, he argues that since the social world is a complex phenomenon it demands a complex discourse to do it justice. Maybe so, but the really important questions here are, does Bourdieu's work have to be *so* complex in its style and presentation, and where does one strike an acceptable balance between necessary complexity and comprehensible communication?

Second, to return to an issue which was alluded to in Chapter Three, there is the epistemological dimension of writing style. The struggle with 'ordinary language' is, in part, an attempt permanently to remind the reader that the account *is* an account, that it is not in any sense a simple description of 'reality'. Bourdieu is trying to indicate the 'status proper to theoretical discourse', which he characterises as 'it all happens as if'.[47] To use another of his own typical formulations, he is trying to prevent the 'reality of the model' becoming confused with the 'model of reality'. He is also signalling the problematic nature of all texts, even 'ordinary descriptions': these are synoptic objectifications, with all of the inherent problems which this entails. Bourdieu's style of writing, therefore, is an aspect of the second step back, the epistemological break with objectification, which we discussed in Chapter Three.

The reader is also the focus of the third point: 'My texts are full of indications meant to stop the reader deforming and simplifying things.' We should, I suppose, be grateful. More the pity, therefore, that, as Bourdieu himself suggests in his next sentence, his readership is often too careless or too stupid to pay attention:

> Unfortunately, these warnings pass unnoticed or else make what I am saying so complicated that readers who read too quickly see neither the little indications nor the big ones and read more or less the exact opposite of what I wanted to say – witness numerous objections that are made to my work.[48]

Further on in the same interview he adds that linguistic and stylistic complexity is necessary in order to protect what he is saying from the misunderstanding which results from the reader's tendency to project onto the text 'his or her prejudices, unreflective opinions and fantasies'.

At this point, it is perhaps worth pausing for reflection. Does Bourdieu *really* view his readership with such suspicion (or contempt)? Does he *really* mean what he says above? There are certainly indications that he did not always feel this way about writing and linguistic style. Consider, for example, the following:

> With the intention of constructing an audaciously novel theory, the author gives little definition of his fundamental concepts, and introduces them in the course of his discussion as a means of meeting difficulties and resolving problems. The reader is not led into an intellectual edifice which was built before him *more geometrico*, but thrown from the beginning straight into a complex system of thought, full of retractions, revisions and innuendos, which does not have the intellectual rigour of a purely analytical construction.[49]

This is not a comment upon Bourdieu (although, in nearly every respect, it could be so). It is Bourdieu criticising, in 1966, Alain Touraine's *Sociologie de l'action*. He has obviously shifted his position somewhat since.

Bourdieu's fourth reason for writing as he does moves the argument more clearly onto political ground. 'False clarity' is often, he argues, an integral part of the 'dominant discourse': this seeks to make things look simpler than they are, and, as the 'discourse of those who think that everything goes without saying', encourages the axiomatic acceptance of the *status quo*. In seeking to subvert and circumvent the conservative 'authority of common sense', Bourdieu is hoping to encourage, at the least, a questioning of the social world. Whether or not this is best achieved by the use of a maximally opaque writing style is, however, another question which is resolutely evaded.

Finally, Bourdieu argues that to produce 'an over-simplified and over-simplifying discourse about the social world' is *inevitably* to provide weapons for the manipulation of the social world 'in dangerous ways'. Here he returns to his argument that social science discourse must be as complex as is demanded by the problem which it is tackling. Once again, the question which is invited is, what counts as *over*-simplification (and, by implication, over-*complication*)? In addition, there is the further question of who defines what is dangerous; and dangerous to *whom*?

In closing this discussion, let us remind ourselves of Bourdieu's argument that academic discourse – its 'elevated style', its sometimes less than delicate abuse, etc. – is a central dimension of the strategies with which academics compete in the struggle for distinction. As I have demonstrated, Bourdieu's writings are cast in the same mould. The same linguistic and presentational devices which he identifies in academic discourse in general are conspicuously present in his own work. In his case, however, these are explained and justified by reference to his epistemological and political goals and purposes.

This is problematic in two respects. First, it is not clear *why* Bourdieu should be so different. Why are his peers and rivals doing one thing, while he is managing – despite the striking similarities of surface appearances – to actually do something radically alternative? Second, upon what grounds is it possible for us to accept Bourdieu's defence of his style of writing and manner of speaking? After all, his own sociology insists that actors' conscious intentions do not and cannot explain their practices. He cannot expect to have his cake and eat it in this respect. This is particularly so when we are dealing with 'official accounts', and Bourdieu's explanations of his own practices, particularly those which are generated in an interview setting (which is where the material drawn upon in the above discussion originates), should probably be classified as such. They may be tactical interventions in the strategies and struggles of his own life and social world, but, following his own arguments, they are not acceptable as explanations of what he does. An explanation, once again by his own account, must probably be sought in Bourdieu's native participation in the French academic field and his, to date extremely successful, pursuit of distinction.

NOTES AND REFERENCES

[1] P. Bourdieu, *Language and Symbolic Power*, ed. J.B. Thompson, Cambridge, Polity (1991).
[2] L.D. Wacquant, 'Towards a reflexive sociology: a workshop with Pierre Bourdieu', *Sociological Theory*, vol. 7 (1989), p. 47.
[3] *Ibid.*, p. 46.
[4] P. Bourdieu, *Language and Symbolic Power*, *op. cit.*, pp. 52–61.
[5] *Ibid.*, pp. 61–5.
[6] *Ibid.*, p. 66.
[7] See: J.L. Austin, *How to do Things with Words*, second edition, Oxford, Clarendon Press (1975).
[8] P. Bourdieu, *Language and Symbolic Power*, *op.cit.*, pp. 107–16.
[9] *Ibid.*, p. 130.
[10] *Ibid.*, pp. 133–6.
[11] *Ibid.*, p. 138.
[12] P. Bourdieu, *The Political Ontology of Martin Heidegger*, Cambridge, Polity (1991), pp. 96–7. See also: P. Bourdieu, *Language and Symbolic Power.*, *op. cit.*, p. 158.
[13] J.B. Thompson, 'Editor's Introduction' to P. Bourdieu, *Language and Symbolic Power*, *op. cit.*, p. 2.
[14] For a variety of approaches within this current sociolinguistic paradigm, see: B. Bernstein, *Class, Codes and Control, Vol 1: Theoretical Studies towards a Sociology of Language*, London, Routledge and Kegan Paul (1971); J.J. Gumperz, *Discourse Strategies*, Cambridge, Cambridge University Press (1982); W. Labov, *Sociolinguistic Patterns*, Philadelphia, University of Pennsylvania Press (1972).
[15] P. Bourdieu, *Homo Academicus*, Cambridge, Polity (1988), p. 11.
[16] *Ibid.*, p. 91.
[17] *Ibid.*, pp. 95–9.

[18] *Ibid.*, p. 114.
[19] P. Bourdieu, *The Political Ontology of Martin Heidegger*, *op.cit.*, p. 88. The quotation which Bourdieu (more or less) paraphrases is from Heidegger's *Poetry, Language, Thought*, New York, Harper Colophon (1975), p. 161.
[20] P. Bourdieu, *Language and Symbolic Power*, *op.cit.*, p. 60.
[21] P. Bourdieu, *The Political Ontology of Martin Heidegger*, *op.cit.*, p. 73.
[22] *Ibid.*, pp. 75–6.
[23] *Ibid.*, p. 76.
[24] P. Bourdieu, *In Other Words*, Cambridge, Polity (1990), p. 142.
[25] P. Bourdieu, *The Political Ontology of Martin Heidegger*, *op.cit.*, p. 41.
[26] *Ibid.*, p. 76.
[27] P. Bourdieu, *Homo Academicus*, *op. cit.*, pp. 194–225.
[28] *Ibid.*, p. 206–7.
[29] L.D. Wacquant, 'Towards a Reflexive Sociology', *op. cit.*, p. 55.
[30] My basic argument here is much the same as C. Wright Mills' when he 'translated' a chunk of Talcott Parsons' *The Social System* into English (see: Mills, *The Sociological Imagination*, New York, Oxford University Press [1959], pp. 27–33). If anything, Bourdieu is a much worse example of systematically compromised intelligibility than Parsons; one wonders what Mills would have made of *Distinction* or *The Logic of Practice*.
[31] P. Bourdieu, *Homo Academicus*, *op. cit.*, p. 149.
[32] *Ibid.*, p. 28.
[33] P. Bourdieu, *In Other Words*, *op. cit.*, p. 123.
[34] As an example of this witness just a few pages, chosen at random, from the English translation of *Outline of a Theory of Practice*: on page 111, the mathematician and philosopher Jean Nicod appears, on 112 it is André Gide and on 113 there is an allusion, in Greek, to Stoic philosophy. None of these contribute anything substantial to the argument.
[35] In one of his discussions of Sartre, for example, the following appear: 'ultra-consistent', 'merely', 'desperate' and 'visceral'. If one were to analyse rigorously the rhetorical tactics and structure of this passage it would, I think, be possible to demonstrate the construction of a systematic misconstrual. Whether it is a knowing one, is difficult to say. See: P.

Bourdieu, *Outline of a Theory of Practice*, Cambridge, Cambridge University Press (1977), pp. 73–6.

[36] F. Barth, *Models of Social Organization*, Occasional Paper No. 23, London, Royal Anthropological Institute (1966).

[37] J.A. Barnes, 'Class and Committees in a Norwegian Island Parish', *Human Relations*, vol. 7 (1954), pp. 39–58.

[38] P. Bourdieu, *In Other Words*, *op. cit.*, p. 27.

[39] P. Bourdieu, *Homo Academicus*, *op. cit.*, p. 24.

[40] *Ibid.*, pp. 16–17.

[41] L.D. Wacquant, 'Towards a Reflexive Sociology', *op. cit.*, p. 44.

[42] *Ibid.*, p. 36.

[43] See, for example: C.C. Lemert, 'Reading French Sociology', in C.C. Lemert (ed.), *French Sociology: Rupture and Renewal since 1968*. New York, Columbia University Press (1981), p. 20; R. Harker, C. Mahar and C. Wilkes (eds), *An Introduction to the Work of Pierre Bourdieu*, London, Macmillan (1990), p. xi.

[44] P. Bourdieu, *The Political Ontology of Martin Heidegger*, *op. cit.*, p. 102.

[45] P. Bourdieu, *In Other Words*, *op. cit.*, p. 40.

[46] *Ibid.*, pp. 51–5.

[47] *Ibid.*, p. 90.

[48] *Ibid.*, p. 52.

[49] J.-D. Reynaud and P. Bourdieu, 'Is a Sociology of Action Possible?', in A. Giddens (ed.), *Positivism and Sociology*, London, Héinemann (1974), p. 101.

8

Using Bourdieu

To some readers this may have seemed an unnecessarily critical appraisal of Bourdieu's work. It could legitimately be argued that a brief introductory text should be positive rather than negative in its orientation. In my defence I can offer three arguments, the first of which is simply that I have accentuated the positive wherever I felt I could. What is more, I offer this as only *one* possible reading of Bourdieu's theory, albeit a plausible one.

Second, in criticising Bourdieu I have attempted to stay within the bounds of his own objectives and ambitions. My strongest criticism of his work is probably that he consistently says he is doing one thing while actually doing something else (and usually something which negates or undermines his stated project). He seeks, for example, to transcend the objectivist–subjectivist dualism while remaining firmly rooted in objectivism. He vociferously rejects determinism while persistently producing deterministic models of social process. He perpetually reminds his readers that his accounts of social life should only be read as models of that social reality – 'it all happens as if' – but is equally consistent in his use of the language of positivist empiricism, which presents his analysis as based in a 'real' material world.

Third, my discussion should be understood as using Bourdieu to think against Bourdieu, in the best tradition of his own work. In this sense, criticism is the sincerest form of flattery.

Which brings me to the positive appreciation of his *oeuvre* which is the appropriate note on which to draw this discussion to a close. As I argued in my introductory remarks, Bourdieu is enormously stimulating, he is 'good to think with'. There are at least two reasons why this should be so. One of them is his reluctance to theorise other than through a research-based engagement with the complexities of social life. The other is his ever-present reflection upon that engagement; upon the effects which doing research in specific ways and contexts have on the theorised products of the research process. The two taken together render it difficult simply to take what he is saying for granted: Bourdieu's work is a constant incitement or encouragement to criticism and further reflection on the reader's part.

Each of these strengths in Bourdieu's work point us in the direction of the epistemological dimensions of his research and theorising. As I have suggested in earlier chapters, Bourdieu's contributions to the epistemology of sociology and anthropology may prove to be the most important of his writings. There are at least three different directions from which this, 'the objectification of objectification', can usefully be approached.

First, there is what Bourdieu describes as 'constructing the object'.[1] It is necessary for the social scientist not to be seduced by the apparent transparency of common-sense models and understandings of the social world. Routine classificatory categories – culture, the family, etc. – are particularly problematic; vigilance is necessary when using notions of this kind in sociological work. They are not, as it were, naturally occurring phenomena which present themselves for study in a direct and unproblematic fashion. Classificatory categories are culturally specific, each with its history and each socially constructed within a network of hierarchical social relations and imbalanced forces of power. Concepts such as these must be used and approached with scepticism (what does this *really* mean?) and care (what are the analytical or theoretical implications of using it?). Each is in conceptual hock to a set of interests served and interests to be served.

The point of view of the sociologist or anthropologist is thus of importance, if in no other sense than that implied in the day-to-day meaning of the expression. Bourdieu acknowledges the politics of social science as well as his own political stance as an individual and attempts to write them into his work. More to the point, he also argues that it is necessary to be aware of the distortions of social reality which are likely to result from the adoption of the stance of the 'objective' observer. Only by the reflexive recognition of the refractive effects of doing research – of objectification – is it possible to allow or control for them.

There is more involved than simply the objective gaze of the researcher, however. There is, in addition, an urgent need to be clear, in our use of them, of the epistemological implications of the techniques and methods of social research. Bourdieu has discussed, for example, synopsis and the ethnographer's recourse to 'official accounts'. He has also discussed the use of statistics in this light. He is insisting upon the researcher's responsibility for the constitution of the social world as an object for analysis and, further, upon the need to be clear about the effects of the methods which we employ in undertaking research upon its results. This is the 'construction of the object' from which no social research can declare its independence.

Second, Bourdieu is keenly aware of the role of style and presentation in the objectification of objectification: this is where the struggle against ordinary language, in which he engages with such enthusiasm, finds its justification. His objective is never to allow the reader to forget, not for a minute, that what he or she is reading is not 'reality' but an account, and what is more, an account which is constructed in particular and specific ways. Whether or not the kind of language which Bourdieu uses is actually justifiable in these terms, and whether or not the price which is exacted in terms of successful communication is too high, is discussed in Chapter Seven, but it is possible to sympathise with Bourdieu's basic argument here.

Third, there is the question of 'participant objectivation', which I have characterised elsewhere as trying to step into the shoes of the actors with whom one's research is concerned. This, too, is a problematic area, particularly inasmuch as, by virtue of the limits to which it is actually possible, it may constrain the researcher to constitute the social world in an impoverished fashion. Participant objectivation is the distrustful empiricist's compromise with the epistemological claims of ethnographic research. Bourdieu suggests that if it is not possible to think as one's research subjects think, it may be possible to (a) imagine oneself doing what they do in the visible world of practice, and/ or (b) extrapolate from how one's own social world is produced as a practical accomplishment to the social world(s) of others. It is a suggestive idea, despite its difficulties, and ties in with an ongoing debate, particularly among feminist social scientists, about the epistemology of empathy.

In insisting that Bourdieu's significance for sociology and anthropology lies primarily in the domain of epistemology, I am not saying that the answers which he provides (or, indeed, the questions which he poses) are, in some sense, 'right'. But he does serve to remind us, in the context of actual empirical research, of the central importance of epistemology to social science and the necessary implication of method in theory, and vice versa. He is, in this sense, a powerful corrective to the gulf which seems to have opened up, especially within sociology (social anthropologists have never embraced this particular error with any enthusiasm), between fundamental theory and the 'hands on' experience of research.

Nor does an emphasis upon Bourdieu's epistemology imply that he has made no other contributions of importance to sociology and anthropology. The other side of Bourdieu's significance lies in his discovery or exploration of substantive problems and research topics which had hitherto been un- or underexamined. Without wishing to propose a definitive or exhaustive catalogue of these, there are some such which are of particular importance inasmuch as they offer fertile ground for further conceptual development and may be of strategic value in the evolution of sociological thinking about the relationship between agency and structure.

An example, and a good place to start, is Bourdieu's implicit recognition that the distinction between conscious thought and the unconscious mind – insofar as the existence of the latter can be posited with any confidence – is not a sharp, either/or separation. Rather, it makes more sense to suggest that conscious and unconscious mental processes lie at opposite ends of a continuum. In between is an area which is, as yet, little considered by sociologists (although behavioural psychologists have given it sustained attention). Inasmuch as it is the domain of habit it is of great sociological importance: if Bourdieu is right, this may be where much socialisation and early childhood learning put down their strongest roots. By an easy extension of his argument, it is also likely to be the source of the potency of processes of institutionalisation.

Related to this point is Bourdieu's argument that culture is encoded in or on the body. What he refers to as habitus and hexis are different dimensions of this embodiment. Now anthropologists have, of course, long been interested in the body, both as a site for cultural expression and as culturally variable with respect to how it is understood and conceptualised. There is also a large and interesting multi-disciplinary literature on non-verbal communication. From another direction, Foucault has written extensively on the uses of the body in social control. Bourdieu's originality lies in his suggestion that some of the power of habituation derives from the role of the body both as a mnemonic device in cultural coding and as an effective vehicle for the less-than-conscious communication or expression of these codes. This potentially provides us with a bridge between the micro-sociology of bodily expression and a wider sociology concerned with the relationship between culture (and by extension, social structure) and agency.

Bourdieu's work also throws into relief the notion of competence in social interaction: how is competence defined and practically accomplished? To refer back to the discussion immediately above, his argument is that both in its learning and its achievement, competence is located largely in the middle hinterland of cognition, neither conscious nor unconscious: if you have to think about what you're doing, it's more likely to be done clumsily or wrongly. Practice, what people do, is not the product of rules, internalised by actors, but is produced by less specific and less definite dispositions. Practice is fundamentally improvisatory, the spinning out over time of the process of adjustment between the constraints, opportunities and demands of specific social fields and the dispositions of the habitus. Whether Bourdieu's discussion of this process is convincing, his work is important because it removes the consideration of social or interactional competence (and incompetence) from the individualist framework of psychology and locates it within a properly social context. It also stresses the role of social definitions and judgements of competence in hierarchical struggles for prestige and status.

These struggles are the final substantive topic in Bourdieu's *oeuvre* which I want to emphasise. The basic idea, that culture is both means and end in competitive struggles for social position, is not new and it is certainly not Bourdieu's. However, Bourdieu's work is important in this respect because of the clarity with which it reveals the cultural struggles of both traditional and modern societies, and because of his systematic exposition of the inter-relatedness of education, cultural consumption and stratification patterns in modern society. In this latter respect, Bourdieu is further to be applauded for his empirical investigations of status categories and relations, dimensions of social inequality and domination which, by comparison, say, with class and social mobility, have been systematically neglected by recent sociology.

These, then, are the epistemological issues, theoretical concerns and substantive topics which Bourdieu has made his own. They offer a challenge and a way forward into further research and theorisation (and, very much following Bourdieu's line, the two should not be allowed to separate). They are also, as I have argued in this book, problematic. In particular, I have suggested that Bourdieu's work is flawed by its internal contradictions and inconsistencies. Inasmuch as he appears, at times, not only to recognise this problem but to embrace it as inevitable this may be an acceptable price to pay for the undoubted strengths and qualities of his work:

> When you want to escape from the world as it is, you can be a musician, or a philosopher, or a mathematician. But how can you escape it as a sociologist? Some people manage to. You just have to write some mathematical formulae, go through a few game-theory exercises, a bit of computer simulation. To be able to see and describe the world as it is, you have to be ready to be always dealing with things that are complicated, confused, impure, uncertain, all of which runs counter to the usual idea of intellectual rigour.[2]

Bourdieu's work, then, despite all of its problems, remains worthy of our most serious attention. Although he is undoubtedly difficult to read, his sociology and anthropology is refreshingly open to criticism precisely because of the pains which he takes to reflect upon what he is doing and to do so, as it were, in the public gaze of the printed page. His weaknesses therefore become his strengths and for that we must applaud him.

NOTES AND REFERENCES

[1] P. Bourdieu, J.-C. Chamboredon and J.-C. Passeron, *The Craft of Sociology: Epistemological Preliminaries*, Berlin, de Gruyter (1991), especially pp. 33–55.
[2] *Ibid.*, p. 259.

Reading Bourdieu

There are a number of routes into Bourdieu's published work. Perhaps the best place to start is his interview with Loic Wacquant: 'Towards a Reflexive Sociology: A Workshop with Pierre Bourdieu', *Sociological Theory*, vol. 7 (1989), pp. 26–63. Following this, you should look at Bourdieu's *In Other Words*, Cambridge, Polity (1990), particularly Chapters 1, 2, 3, 8 and 13. Taken together, these provide, in his own words, accessible general introductions to Bourdieu's work. Another important piece which does a similar job and has not yet been anthologised is, '*Vive la crise*! For Heterodoxy in Social Science', *Theory and Society*, vol. 17 (1988), pp. 773–87.

Following this, there are some more specialised books and articles which are written in his most accessible style. My personal favourite is *Algeria 1960*, Cambridge, Cambridge University Press (1979); this includes the piece on the Kabyle house, which is also available in *The Logic of Practice*, Cambridge, Polity (1990), pp. 271–83. This is a classic example of structuralist analysis and not to be missed. Another paper which is deserving of classic status also provides the best short introduction to Bourdieu's sociology of education and his theory of social and cultural reproduction: 'Cultural Reproduction and Social Reproduction', originally published in R. Brown (ed.), *Knowledge, Education and Cultural Change*, London, Tavistock (1973), can also be found in J. Karabel and A.H. Halsey (eds), *Power and Ideology in Education*, New York, Oxford University Press (1977). A good, brief introduction to some of Bourdieu's epistemological arguments can be found in the 'Introduction' to Bourdieu, L. Boltanski, R. Castel and J.C. Chamboredon, *Photography*, Cambridge, Polity (1991). Lastly, there is *Language and Symbolic Power*, Cambridge, Polity (1991): the 'Introduction' and Chapters 1, 3 and 11 are particularly useful and unusually straightforward for Bourdieu.

Having come this far, the only thing to do is to proceed to attack the major works. There is little point in reading both *Outline of a Theory of Practice*, Cambridge, Cambridge University Press (1977) and *The Logic of Practice*, Cambridge, Polity (1990). My advice would be to read *Logic*. The other essential books are *Reproduction in Education, Society and Culture*, London, Sage, second edition (1990), *Distinction*, London, Routledge and Kegan Paul (1984) and *Homo Academicus*, Cambridge, Polity (1988). The other major publications which are available in English translation are largely of specialist or historical interest.

Finally there are the commentaries on Bourdieu's work. I can particularly recommend J.B. Thompson, 'Editor's Introduction' in Bourdieu's *Language and Symbolic Power*; R.W. Connell, *Which Way is Up?*, Sydney, George Allen and Unwin Australia (1983), pp. 140–61; R. Sharp, *Knowledge, Ideology and the Politics of Schooling*, London, Routledge and Kegan Paul (1980), pp. 66–76; R.K. Harker, 'On Reproduction, Habitus and Education', *British Journal of Sociology of Education*, vol. 5 (1984), pp. 117–27; A. Honneth, 'The Fragmented World of Symbolic Forms', *Theory, Culture and Society*, vol. 3, no. 3 (1986), pp. 55–66; J. Frow, 'Accounting for Tastes', *Cultural Studies*, vol. 1 (1987), pp. 59–73; L. Wacquant, 'Symbolic Violence and the Making of the French Agriculturalist', *Australia and New Zealand Journal of Sociology*, vol. 23 (1987), pp. 65–88.

On a grander scale there are two other book-length discussions of Bourdieu available. Offering very different approaches, each is more positive about Bourdieu's work than I have been and you should, in fairness, look at both: R. Harker, C. Mahar and C. Wilkes (eds), *An Introduction to the Work of Pierre Bourdieu*,

London, Macmillan (1990), and D. Robbins, *The Work of Pierre Bourdieu*, Buckingham, Open University Press (1991). An alternative suggested approach to reading Bourdieu's work can be found in L. Wacquant, 'Towards a Reflexive Sociology', *op. cit.*, pp. 55–6.

Name index

Subject index